HOW TO
FEED
YOURSELF

THIS COOKBOOK

was designed to give you exactly what you
need to feed yourself . . . depending on what's
in your fridge, what you're craving, or what's
happening in your life.

DO SOME SOUL-SEARCHING AND FLIP AHEAD.

SPOON
UNIVERSITY

HOW TO
FEED
YOURSELF

100 FAST, CHEAP, AND RELIABLE RECIPES FOR COOKING
WHEN YOU DON'T KNOW WHAT YOU'RE DOING

HARMONY BOOKS
NEW YORK

RECIPES

THERE'S MORE! ⟿→

WHO ARE WE TO WRITE A COOKBOOK?

AN INTRODUCTION

We had no idea what we were doing when we started this thing in 2013.

The collective "we" in this introduction is us, Sarah and Kenzie, the cofounders of Spoon University (hey!), and the "thing" was Spoon. You might know Spoon as the food media brand, the campus publication, or that random Instagram account you follow. But before Spoon had millions of fans, or a real office, we were twenty-one years old, sitting on the floor, surrounded by discounted snacks. See right for proof.

That was the night we came up with the idea for Spoon: a food publication written for college students who didn't know how to feed themselves, by college students who were trying to figure out food for the first time, too. From that humbling moment on, we've dedicated our lives to helping young people eat better, and, on a personal level, growing our careers. Ya know, real adult stuff. It turns out that there's one trick to becoming an adult that most people don't talk about— **you have to fake it till you make it.**

That's what this book is all about: faking it in the kitchen until one day you can actually cook on your own and feed yourself. Picking up this book, reading it, owning it is just your first step.

For us, faking it on our way to success started with posting recruitment fliers around Northwestern University for our food magazine that didn't actually exist yet. We weren't experts, but we knew we could help ourselves and others figure out food by getting a group of smart people together. After pretending like we already had a food magazine and inviting people to attend the next meeting, fifty people showed up to share what food topics they wanted to talk about. By the end of the year, a hundred people were on staff. We had struck a chord and it was weird . . . and exciting as hell.

We were talking about food in a way people hadn't before. Spoon wasn't just about perfecting your guac recipe, but the wholeness you feel gathered around the bowl with your squad. By connecting with our food, we were connecting with our lives and finding our people. And just when we were falling in love with our food community, students from around the country began emailing us to start their own chapter. We built them sites of their own and continued to watch our baby grow.

Around this time, during senior year, we had a choice to get a "real job" or run with Spoon. We probably would have been damn good entry-level employees at a magazine, but we decided to take the more uncertain path: try to turn Spoon into a business and, accordingly, give ourselves the fake-but-now-real titles of CEO and CTO. Suddenly, we became C-level executives of a media startup. We moved to NYC, shared a tiny apartment in the East Village, and soon realized not everything is as easy as giving yourself a fancy title.

We started pitching investors the idea of Spoon, "a food tech company, the fastest-growing food brand for the next generation," and basically everyone said no. No, you're not big enough—you need a million monthly visitors. No, we won't give you money—you don't know what you're doing. Just, no. It sucked, but we also started getting a clearer idea of what "no" really meant: prove it and make it happen.

That's when we joined Techstars, an accelerator program (aka startup boot camp), and after twelve intense weeks of working our asses off, we built a big enough audience to turn investors' no's into yeses and raised two million dollars.

We made it to the next step, which was to hire a team of people. Never having interviewed or hired anyone before (and never having been interviewed or hired ourselves), this was a true test in how well we could pull off being heads of HR.

One of the people who joined the team in our hiring spree was Rachel. She was a recent college grad who was a former summer intern, had excelled at her local Spoon chapter at the University of Illinois, and happened to have 70,000 personal Pinterest followers. We were looking for a social media editor, figured she must know more than we do about social, and gave her the offer. However, after a month of her working with us, we started to think we had made a mistake.

Rachel still had a lot to learn, and the pressure of growing fast was intense. There came a point where we told Rachel that if things didn't improve soon, we'd have to find someone else. The next day, she sat us down for a meeting. She admitted that she lacked the knowledge and experience we were looking for, but she promised she would become what we needed, if we could just give her three things: time, support, and our confidence in her.

In so many ways she represented the reasons we started Spoon: believe in yourself, put in the hard work, and fake it till you make it. We agreed to give her time and support. And Rachel figured it out: that year we went from 25,000 fans to more than one million, and she later became our head of editorial. And now Rachel has written this book.

After two more years of going for it, we achieved a huge milestone: in 2017, Spoon was acquired by Scripps Networks Interactive—now Discovery Inc.—home to Food Network. It's a bittersweet (and pretty grueling) process to sell your company, but being a part of Scripps meant the kind of resources and support we always dreamed of were available. We're now able to do incredible things, such as work with the Food Network culinary team to test recipes for this cookbook, and help over 10,000 students across the country grow their own food communities. Spoon is making an impact in ways we always knew it could back in 2013.

So what does it really mean to make it? We don't think there's a time in life where you sit back and say, "Ah, I've made it." Life is a constant hustle of setting goals and hitting them and celebrating milestones. There are many moments of "making it." But milestones don't just fall into your lap. It takes hard work, commitment, and the confidence to fake it until you make your dreams a reality.

The same thing applies to cooking. We've heard so many people over the years say, "I can't cook" as an excuse to not start making their own food. Whether you want to be independent in the kitchen, eat a little healthier, or simply know how to cook chicken breast, this cookbook is your first step to learning how to feed yourself. Just go for it, like we did! Even if your dishes don't look like ours (which they probably won't—we had food stylists involved here), it's still food that you made with your bare hands, and that's pretty awesome. We're here to cheer you on until you're crying tears of joy while cutting onions and sprinkling turmeric into your pasta like a seasoning god. Just tell yourself that you're an amazing cook, or an amazing [fill in the blank], and someday, you probably will be.

Never forks,
Sarah + Kenzie

HOW TO USE THIS COOKBOOK

THE BASICS

You know how cookbooks usually start with a pantry section that tells you all the things you need to buy before you even get started? You probably always flip past those pages to get to the good stuff, and we do, too. So we decided to save some trees and skip all that. But we do want to explain real fast our philosophy in creating these recipes for you, and lay out some ground rules for using them to their fullest potential.

We are assuming that you, like us, are starting in a tiny kitchen, the kind where your oven doubles as pan storage. You've probably inherited a hodgepodge of utensils from generous relatives and/or former roommates. Maybe the place where you cut your veggies is the same place where you work on your laptop. Maybe you've never cut veggies before. Don't worry—you've found your people here.

We developed these recipes for utmost flexibility, with no special equipment and easy-to-find (read: cheap . . . but healthy!) ingredients. We aren't assuming you know anything about cooking, because *we* didn't when we first started. But you probably know a thing or two about eating and only want to put fresh, delicious, healthy-but-not-too-healthy food in your body. That's where this book comes in.

At the most basic level, to get started you need some sharp knives, a cutting board, an ovenproof skillet, a large pot, a baking sheet, a spatula, a slotted spoon, and a couple of bowls of varying sizes. Some recipes call for a hand mixer or a food processor, but you can make do by beating vigorously with a fork most of the time. Overall, we're assuming you've got an oven with a stovetop and a broiler, a microwave, a fridge, and a sink . . . and that's about it.

We know you aren't really eating breakfast at the break of dawn, lunch at noon, and dinner at six. While we encourage three meals a day, sometimes life doesn't stick to an agenda. So instead of organizing the book by meals, we chose the nine ingredients you're most likely to lean on (eggs, chicken, pasta, fish, potatoes, toast, grains, veggies, and bananas) and will show you all the different ways to fry, boil, mash, and bake them.

Some of these recipes call for meat and dairy. If you're going dairy-free for a month or cooking for your vegetarian friend, many of these dishes are forgiving enough for easy swaps, and we'll let you know where swapping regular dairy out for vegan or nondairy options work. We can't promise that everything will come out exactly the same if you switch out the cheese for tofu, or cow's milk for soy, but don't be afraid to experiment with the ingredients that work for you. Be creative and improvise. That's the key to getting comfortable in the kitchen.

We kept these recipes simple enough for you to remember instinctively because that's what being a real person in the kitchen is really all about— having those fallback recipes that are there for you no matter what.

HOW TO COOK ALL OF THE EGGS

We believe in being resourceful: spending less money on protein, turning a carton of eggs into eight different meals, and indulging in the glory of the yolk. That's why we're kicking off your journey of going for it in your tiny-ass kitchen with eggs. Confining eggs to the breakfast category ends right now.

MICROWAVED

1 Coat a microwave-safe mug with nonstick cooking spray. Crack in 2 large eggs, add a splash of water, and beat with a fork until frothy. 2 Season with salt and pepper. Microwave for 1 minute. 3 Stir, then microwave for 45 seconds to 1 minute more. Let sit for 1 minute before eating.

SCRAMBLED

1 In a medium bowl, beat 3 eggs with 2 tablespoons of milk. Season with salt and pepper. 2 Melt 1 tablespoon of butter in a large nonstick skillet over medium heat. When the butter starts to sizzle, swirl to coat the skillet, then pour in the eggs. 3 Cook for a few seconds, then stir slowly until the eggs are just the way you like them, 2 to 6 minutes.

POACHED

1 Bring a medium saucepan filled with 2 inches of water to a low simmer (just a few bubbles every few seconds) over medium heat. 2 Add 1½ tablespoons of distilled white vinegar. Crack 2 to 4 eggs into separate mugs. Stir the water clockwise to create a whirlpool, then slip the eggs into the water one at a time. 3 Cook until the whites are set but the yolks are still runny, about 4 minutes. 4 Transfer to a paper towel-lined plate with a slotted spoon.

BOILED

1 Put uncracked eggs in a saucepan and cover with water by 1 inch. Bring to a boil, then cover and remove from the heat. 2 Let the eggs sit in the hot water for 4 minutes for soft-boiled, 8 minutes for medium, or 12 minutes for hard-boiled. 3 Drain and cool under cold running water, then peel.

FRIED

1 Brush a nonstick skillet with 1 teaspoon of oil. Crack in 2 eggs, then season with salt and pepper. 2 Cook over medium heat until the edges of the whites are set, about 1 minute. 3 Cover the skillet and reduce the heat to low. Cook for 4 minutes for runny, 5 minutes for medium, or 6 minutes for hard. For over easy, flip the eggs when whites are set and cook as above.

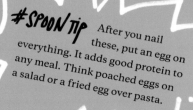

#SPOON TIP After you nail these, put an egg on everything. It adds good protein to any meal. Think poached eggs on a salad or a fried egg over pasta.

MICROWAVED

BOILED

POACHED

SCRAMBLED

FRIED

Put an Egg on It Personal Pizza

BEST FOR **trying your hand at homemade pizza.**

SERVES 1
ACTIVE TIME: 20 minutes
TOTAL TIME: 20 minutes
LEVEL: Easy

Ditch the frozen pizza and take on this recipe that calls for gooey white cheeses and cracking an egg on top. If you chicken out baking it with the egg, you can always cook the egg separately and add it on top. Fry like no one's watching.

6 ounces store-bought pizza dough

1 teaspoon olive oil, plus more for stretching the dough

½ cup shredded low-moisture mozzarella cheese

2 tablespoons ricotta cheese

1 tablespoon grated Parmesan cheese

Kosher salt

Red pepper flakes

1 large egg

3 or 4 fresh basil leaves

1. Preheat the oven to 450°F with a baking sheet on the bottom rack.

2. Lightly brush the dough with the oil and stretch it on a square of parchment paper on another flat or inverted baking sheet into an 8-inch round. Sprinkle with the mozzarella and dollop the ricotta all around. Sprinkle with the Parmesan, salt, and red pepper flakes, to taste. Using oven mitts, slide the parchment off its baking sheet onto the preheated baking sheet in the oven and bake until puffed and golden on the edges, 4 to 5 minutes.

3. Crack the egg into a small bowl. Quickly pull out the oven rack and pour the egg on top of the pizza. Continue to bake until the egg is cooked to your liking, about 4 minutes for a slightly runny yolk. To serve, top with torn basil leaves and cut the pizza into wedges.

#SPOON TIP **SHOP FOR DOUGH:** You can usually find pizza dough in the refrigerated section of the grocery store near the cheese or in a tube by the biscuits. Or if you're feeling savvy, try your favorite pizza joint, and ask them to sell you a ball of dough.

Veggie-Loaded Frittata

BEST FOR **when you need something filling, but you only have eggs.**

SERVES 4
ACTIVE TIME: 20 minutes
TOTAL TIME: 20 minutes
LEVEL: Easy

Trust your instincts. If you think your veggies are about to go bad, they probably are. Turn them into this bomb frittata, something a little more substantial and satisfying.

2 tablespoons olive oil

1 medium onion, sliced

2 cups total of the following vegetables, in any combination: chopped bell peppers, sliced white or cremini mushrooms, chopped zucchini

2 cups packed leafy greens, such as baby spinach or kale

Kosher salt and freshly ground black pepper

8 large eggs

¼ cup half-and-half or any kind of milk (the fatter, the better)

2 tablespoons chopped fresh herbs, such as basil, parsley, and/or chives

1½ cups total of the following shredded cheeses, in any combination: Cheddar, Monterey Jack, Swiss, or low-moisture mozzarella

1. Preheat the broiler, with a rack positioned about 8 inches below the heat source.

2. Heat the olive oil in a medium ovenproof nonstick skillet over medium heat. When the oil is hot and starts to shimmer, add the onion and cook, stirring occasionally, until golden, 6 to 7 minutes. Add the vegetables and cook, stirring occasionally, until tender and golden in places, 4 to 5 minutes. Add the leafy greens and season with ¼ teaspoon salt and several grinds of pepper. Toss and cook until the greens are wilted and any liquid in the skillet has evaporated, 2 to 3 minutes. Remove the skillet from the heat.

3. Combine the eggs, half-and-half, ½ teaspoon salt, and several grinds of pepper in a medium bowl. Beat with a fork to combine, then stir in the chopped herbs and 1 cup of the shredded cheese. Return the skillet to medium-low heat and pour the egg mixture over the vegetables. Cook, without stirring, until the bottom and sides are set, 4 to 5 minutes, adjusting the heat if needed so it doesn't brown too fast. Sprinkle with the remaining ½ cup cheese. Move the skillet to the broiler and broil until the top is browned and the center is just set, 2 to 3 minutes. (If the top browns before the center is set, turn off the oven and let the frittata finishing cooking in the residual heat for a few extra minutes.)

4. Let the frittata sit in the pan for about 5 minutes. Carefully invert it onto a cutting board and cut into wedges. Serve warm or at room temperature.

HOW TO TAKE CONTROL OF YOUR BROILER

Broiling is simply applying dry heat to the surface of foods. It's good to meet your broiler because it helps you quickly melt cheese and brown food. A toaster oven can also broil food like a champ.

FIND IT FIRST

Your broiler can be on the top or bottom of your oven. If you don't know, turn it on and wait a minute; you'll be able to tell where the heat is coming from.

ONE SIZE FITS ALL

It's either on or off, but it still needs to preheat, like any normal oven.

ALWAYS SET A TIMER

Your food can go from flame-kissed to burnt in less than a minute, so keep an eye on your food.

SAY NO TO MOISTURE

Make sure to pat foods dry or they'll steam instead of brown.

FOR TOP BROILERS

The sweet spot is 4 inches from the broiler, but the standard height on the oven rack is 3 to 5 inches. Place food on the highest rack and keep a close eye.

Egg in the Hole

BEST FOR 2 a.m. late night or 2 p.m. breakfast.

SERVES 1
ACTIVE TIME: 10 minutes
TOTAL TIME: 10 minutes
LEVEL: Easy

Making this creation lives and dies with the technique of cutting out a hole from a slice of bread, cracking an egg within the hole, and SUCCESSFULLY flipping it over. Just know that a lot of smoke coming from your pan means you should've flipped it thirty seconds ago.

1 slice whole wheat bread

2 teaspoons olive oil

1 large egg

Kosher salt and freshly ground black pepper

BBQ sauce, ketchup, hot sauce, or red pepper flakes (optional)

1. Cut a hole in the center of the bread with a 2-inch round cookie cutter.
2. Heat the olive oil in a medium nonstick skillet over medium-high heat. Add both the slice of bread and the cutout to the skillet. Crack the egg into the hole in the bread.
3. Reduce the heat to medium and fry until the egg white is set, the bread lifts up easily from the skillet, and the underside is golden brown, 4 to 5 minutes. Carefully turn the bread over with a spatula and cook the egg to the desired doneness. Turn the cutout over and cook until the underside is golden brown, 1 to 2 minutes.
4. Serve the egg in the hole with the bread cutout for dipping and BBQ sauce, ketchup, hot sauce, or red pepper flakes, if desired.

#SPOON TIP Because you probably don't have a cookie cutter, use a glass or shot glass to make the cutout in the bread.

Egg Salad That's Easy on the Eyes

BEST FOR **when you need to finish that bag of greens.**

SERVES 1
ACTIVE TIME: 20 minutes
TOTAL TIME: 20 minutes
LEVEL: Easy

Try this take on salad, which includes soft-boiled eggs, biscuit croutons, and kale. It's kind of like a breakfast salad, but we won't judge you for when you eat it.

1 slice of any bread or a biscuit, cut into cubes

3 tablespoons olive oil

Kosher salt and freshly ground black pepper

1 large egg

2 slices deli ham, cut into small squares

4 cups packed baby kale

4 or 5 grape or cherry tomatoes, halved

¼ small red onion, thinly sliced

1 tablespoon cider vinegar

3 tablespoons shredded Cheddar cheese

1. Preheat the oven to 350°F.
2. Toss the bread cubes with 1 tablespoon of the olive oil in a medium bowl. Spread on a baking sheet and bake until crisp and golden, tossing once or twice, 8 to 10 minutes. Season with salt and pepper.
3. Put the uncracked egg in a small pot and add water to cover by 1 inch. Bring to a boil, then cover and remove from the heat. Let the egg continue to cook in the hot water: 4 minutes for soft-boiled, 8 minutes for medium, or 12 minutes for hard-boiled. Drain and cool under running water.
4. Heat 1 tablespoon of the oil in a skillet over medium heat. When the oil starts to shimmer, add the ham and cook, tossing occasionally, until crisp, about 2 minutes. Remove the skillet from the heat and transfer the ham to a paper towel–lined plate with a slotted spoon or fork, leaving the oil in the skillet.
5. To assemble the salad, pile the kale in a shallow bowl and top with the tomatoes, red onion, ham, and croutons. Peel and halve the egg; place on top of the salad.
6. Return the skillet to the stovetop over medium heat and whisk in the remaining oil and the vinegar; season with salt and pepper. Drizzle the warm dressing over the salad, sprinkle with the cheese, and serve.

Not Your Average BEC

BEST FOR when you need to recover but don't wanna leave your apartment for breakfast.

SERVES 1
ACTIVE TIME: 15 minutes
TOTAL TIME: 15 minutes
LEVEL: Easy

Think cheesy scrambled eggs and crispy bacon sandwiched between two waffles and sautéed in hot maple syrup. It's the best bacon-egg-and-cheese hangover breakfast of our generation, and it's all yours. If you can imagine it, you can make it.

2 round toaster waffles

3 slices bacon

1 tablespoon (3 teaspoons) unsalted butter

2 tablespoons maple syrup

2 slices Cheddar or American cheese

2 large eggs, beaten

Kosher salt and freshly ground black pepper

1. Toast the waffles according to the package directions. Meanwhile, cook the bacon in a medium nonstick skillet over medium heat, turning occasionally, until crisp, about 4 minutes. Drain the bacon on a plate lined with paper towels.

2. Pour off the fat from the skillet, leaving just enough to coat the bottom. Return the skillet to medium heat and add 2 teaspoons of the butter and the maple syrup. Cook, swirling the pan, until the butter has melted and the mixture is bubbling, about 1 minute. Add the waffles and press lightly to coat one side in the maple butter. Cook until the underside is caramelized on the ridges (aka brown and crackly), about 1 minute. Flip and press lightly. Top each waffle with a slice of cheese and cook until it begins to melt, about 1 minute. Transfer the cheesy waffles to a plate.

3. Quickly wipe the skillet clean with a paper towel and return it to medium heat. Melt the remaining teaspoon butter in the skillet, add the beaten eggs, and season with salt and pepper. Cook, stirring, until the eggs are set to your liking, about 2 minutes for medium. Fold the eggs to fit the size of the waffle. Add the bacon to one waffle, top with the eggs, and cover with the second waffle.

4. Repeat steps until you and your roomies or overnight guest are full.

You'll probably need a fork and knife to eat this thing. Or gloves.

Easy Eggs Benny

BEST FOR when you don't want to deal with the brunch crowd.

SERVES 2
ACTIVE TIME: 30 minutes
TOTAL TIME: 30 minutes
LEVEL: Medium

We'll show you how to master this classic breakfast dish with an easy hollandaise for when you'd rather brunch solo and stay on the couch in your pj's. Just go for it. You miss 100% of the sauces you don't make, ya know.

FOR THE SAUCE:

3 large egg yolks

1 tablespoon hot water

1 tablespoon fresh lemon juice

8 tablespoons (1 stick) unsalted butter, melted

Kosher salt and freshly ground black pepper

FOR THE EGGS:

1½ tablespoons distilled white vinegar

4 large eggs

2 English muffins

4 slices tomato

Cayenne pepper or paprika, for serving (optional)

1. Make the hollandaise first so your food is hot when you're ready to serve it: Put the egg yolks, hot water, and lemon juice in a blender and blend for 1 minute. While the blender is running, slowly pour in the melted butter. Season with salt and pepper.

2. Poach the eggs: Fill a skillet with 2 inches of water and bring it to a low simmer (just a few bubbles every few seconds) over medium heat. Add the vinegar. In separate mugs, crack the whole eggs. Stir the water clockwise to create a whirlpool, then slip the eggs into the water one at a time.

Cook until the whites are set but the yolks are still runny, about 4 minutes. Transfer to a paper towel–lined plate with a slotted spoon.

3. Toast the English muffins. Top each English muffin half with a slice of tomato and a poached egg. Top with some hollandaise and sprinkle with cayenne or paprika, if you'd like.

#SPOON TIP

GO OLD-SCHOOL: Swap out the tomato for Canadian bacon or lox.

NO BLENDER? NO PROB: If you don't have a blender, whisk the eggs, hot water, and lemon juice until pale yellow. Drizzle in the butter, a little at a time, whisking until each addition is fully incorporated. Season with salt and pepper.

4 p.m. Hangover Hash

BEST FOR when you want a hearty breakfast, but your energy level is low.

SERVES 2
ACTIVE TIME: 35 minutes
TOTAL TIME: 35 minutes
LEVEL: Easy

This is your "work with what you have" dish, aka "throw all breakfasty foods into a skillet and make a meal out of it." We'll walk you through cooking your potatoes and sausage to crispy perfection and finishing it off with baked eggs nestled all cozy in the hash.

1 pound Yukon Gold or russet potatoes (about 2 medium)

3 tablespoons unsalted butter

2 fully cooked sausage links (kielbasa, andouille, chicken and apple, or any kind you like), cut into small cubes (about 6 ounces)

1 small onion, chopped

1 small red (or any color) bell pepper, chopped

1 teaspoon paprika or smoked paprika

Kosher salt and freshly ground black pepper

4 large eggs

2 scallions, chopped

Hot sauce, for serving

1. Preheat the oven to 400°F.
2. Prick the potatoes in four or five places with a fork and microwave in a bowl, rotating halfway through, until almost tender, 5 to 6 minutes. Let cool, 5 to 10 minutes. Peel and cut into ½-inch chunks.
3. Melt the butter in a medium nonstick ovenproof skillet over medium heat. Add the sausage and cook until the edges begin to crisp, about 2 minutes. Add the onion and bell pepper and cook, stirring occasionally, until almost tender, 4 to 5 minutes. Add the potatoes, sprinkle with the paprika, and season with salt and black pepper. Stir to coat the hash in the seasonings. Press the hash down with a spatula or big spoon and cook until the bottom starts to crisp, about 4 minutes. Flip portions of the hash in batches, pressing down until the hash is crispy all over and the vegetables are tender, about 4 minutes more.
4. Make four indentations in the hash with the back of a serving spoon and crack an egg into each. Season the eggs with salt and black pepper. Transfer the skillet to the oven and bake until the eggs are done to your liking, 4 to 6 minutes for firm whites with still-runny yolks. Sprinkle with the scallions and serve immediately, with hot sauce alongside.

#SPOON TIP WHEN SELECTING ONIONS AT THE STORE: Look for those that are firm and dry with a shiny, crackling outer skin. Avoid those with dark spots, as this can indicate mold, and those with excessively strong odors, 'cause this might be a sign of rotting. You should cry when you cut them—not when you smell them.

All-Day Breakfast Tacos

BEST FOR when you have a full apartment of people who need to be fed.

MAKES 8 TACOS
ACTIVE TIME: 25 minutes
TOTAL TIME: 25 minutes
LEVEL: Easy

These babies will bring you that same amazing flavor of authentic Austin, Texas, tacos with scrambled eggs, tortillas, and easy-to-find store-bought ingredients like salsa and refried beans WITHOUT, you know, traveling. This is a flexible recipe. Don't eat sausage? Leave it out. You do you.

8 corn tortillas (most are about 6 inches)

½ cup sour cream

2 tablespoons chopped fresh cilantro

1 (15.5-ounce) can refried beans

1 tablespoon olive oil

8 ounces fresh (Mexican) chorizo, casings removed

6 large eggs

¼ cup whole milk

Kosher salt and freshly ground black pepper

½ cup shredded Mexican blend, Cheddar, or pepper Jack cheese

Red and/or green salsa, for serving

Diced avocado, for serving

Pickled jalapeño slices, for serving

Lime wedges, for serving

1. Preheat the oven to 350°F.
2. Wrap the tortillas in foil and heat them in the oven until warmed through, about 10 minutes. Meanwhile, mix the sour cream and cilantro in a small bowl. Microwave the beans in a microwave-safe bowl according to the package instructions.
3. Heat the olive oil in a nonstick skillet over medium heat. When the oil starts to shimmer, add the chorizo and cook, crumbling the meat with a wooden spoon, until cooked through and browned, 4 to 5 minutes. Transfer the chorizo to a bowl and pour off all but about 1 tablespoon of the fat from the skillet.
4. Return the skillet to medium heat. Beat the eggs, milk, ½ teaspoon of salt, and several grinds of black pepper in a medium bowl. Pour the eggs into the skillet. Cook for a few seconds, then stir slowly until the eggs are cooked just the way you like them, 2 to 6 minutes. Sprinkle the eggs with the cheese in the last minute and stir to combine.
5. Remove the tortillas from the oven. Serve the eggs, beans, and chorizo in the warm tortillas, topped with salsa, avocado, and pickled jalapeños, and lime wedges on the side.

DON'T BE A

CHICKEN

A GUIDE TO MAKING CHICKEN NOT BLAND

There's a time and place to be naked, and your chicken is not it. If you tend to make chicken almost every night, these marinades, dips, and breadings are your new best friends. All you need is a pound of skinless chicken breasts and to read on.

marinades

Just pour the marinade into a quart-size zip-top plastic bag, add up to 1 pound of boneless, skinless chicken breasts (about 2 breasts) and press out all the air to seal. Marinate for at least 2 hours or up to overnight. Season with salt and pepper right before cooking.

CILANTRO-LIME

1 cup packed fresh cilantro leaves
¼ cup olive oil
Zest of 1 lime and 3 tablespoons fresh lime juice
2 tablespoons honey or agave nectar

Combine the cilantro, olive oil, lime zest, lime juice, and honey in a blender or food processor and blend until smooth. (Bonus ingredient: Add a shot of tequila to the marinade for a boozy kick.)

MAPLE-CIDER

¼ cup olive oil
2 tablespoons maple syrup
2 tablespoons cider vinegar
1 teaspoon smoked paprika or regular sweet paprika (smoked is great here, if you have it)

Whisk together the olive oil, maple syrup, vinegar, and paprika in a small bowl.

BEER–BROWN SUGAR

1 cup beer of your choice
5 garlic cloves, finely chopped
2 tablespoons light brown sugar
1 tablespoon fresh thyme leaves, chopped, or 1 teaspoon dried, crumbled

Whisk together the beer, garlic, brown sugar, and thyme in a small bowl.

#SPOON TIP Don't forget to refrigerate the chicken while marinating or it will go bad. Thirty minutes before cooking, remove it from the fridge and bring to room temperature.

BEER–BROWN SUGAR

MAPLE-CIDER

CILANTRO-LIME

dipping sauces

These sauces work well with both plain or marinated cooked chicken breasts. Just whisk them in a small bowl and serve with your chicken. You can keep these covered in the fridge for up to 2 days as long as you stir well before serving.

SRIRACHA-LIME KETCHUP

½ cup ketchup
Zest and juice of 1 large lime
2 teaspoons sriracha

ORANGE MUSTARD

¼ cup grainy Dijon mustard
¼ cup orange marmalade
1 tablespoon chopped fresh chives

PESTO MAYONNAISE

½ cup mayonnaise
2 tablespoons prepared pesto
1 tablespoon fresh lemon juice
Freshly ground black pepper

GINGER-SESAME-SOY SAUCE

Juice of 1 orange (about ⅓ cup;
    store-bought is fine)
2 tablespoons soy sauce
2 teaspoons sesame oil
1 teaspoon finely grated fresh ginger

breadings

Getting creative is the dream, but start simple with thin, lil' chicken cutlets.

To make crumbs: Start with 2 to 2½ cups coarsely crumbled potato chips, tortilla chips, cornflakes, orange cheese crackers (i.e., Goldfish), or pretzels. Pulse in a food processor to make light bread crumbs (about the texture of panko) or seal the crumbles in a zip-top plastic bag and crush with a rolling pin or wine bottle. You should get about 1 heaping cup of crumbs.

CRISPY CHICKEN CUTLETS

1 cup all-purpose flour
2 large eggs
Kosher salt and freshly ground black
    pepper
1 cup bread crumbs of your choice,
    or ¾ cup panko mixed with ¼ cup
    grated Parmesan cheese
1 pound thinly sliced boneless, skinless
    chicken cutlets (about 4 pieces)
Vegetable or olive oil, for cooking

[1] Spread the flour in a shallow bowl. Beat the eggs with a pinch of salt in a second shallow bowl. Spread the bread crumbs in a third shallow bowl. [2] Season the cutlets with salt and pepper. Heat a thin layer of oil in a large nonstick skillet over medium heat. One at a time, dredge (aka dip) the chicken in the flour, then the egg, letting the excess drip back into the bowl. Finally, dredge the cutlets in the crumbs, patting gently to help coat. [3] When the oil starts to shimmer, add the cutlets to the pan. Cook, turning once and adjusting the heat if needed to keep them from scorching, until the cutlets are golden and cooked through, 2 to 3 minutes per side. Drain on a paper towel-lined plate before serving.

#SPOON Tip You can crush anything into crumbs and use as breading, except stay away from sugary ones, like frosted cornflakes, which will burn.

HOW TO COOK CHICKEN BREASTS

Most nights, you're not cooking a whole bird or even dealing with the wings. Follow along with chicken-breast cooking that works best for you tonight. Then continue on for ideal weeknight dinners, easy lunch options, and other not-boring chicken ideas.

MICROWAVE POACHED

Kosher salt
1 boneless, skinless chicken breast
(8 to 9 ounces)

1 Put 2½ cups water and a generous pinch of salt in a microwave-safe bowl. 2 Microwave for 2 minutes, then carefully add the chicken breast. 3 Microwave for another 6 minutes; let the chicken cool in the liquid for 5 minutes. 4 Drain and shred with a fork or slice.

ROASTED

Olive oil or nonstick cooking spray
4 boneless, skinless chicken breasts
(8 to 9 ounces each)
Kosher salt and freshly ground black
pepper

1 Preheat the oven to 400°F. 2 Coat a baking sheet with oil. 3 Coat the chicken on all sides with oil and season with salt and pepper. 4 Roast the chicken on the baking sheet until done and the juices run clear, not pink, when you pierce the chicken with a knife, 30 to 35 minutes. If you have an instant-read food thermometer, the thickest part of the breast should register 165°F. Let the chicken rest for 5 minutes before slicing.

GRILLED

2 boneless, skinless chicken breasts
(8 to 9 ounces each)
Kosher salt and freshly ground black
pepper
Canola oil, for brushing

1 Heat a grill to medium or heat a grill pan over medium heat. Season the chicken with salt and pepper. 2 Once the grill or grill pan is hot, oil the grates or the pan with a paper towel. Add the chicken and cook until cooked through, 15 to 18 minutes, flipping once halfway through the cooking time. 3 Let rest for 5 minutes before slicing.

POACHED

2 boneless, skinless chicken breasts
(8 to 9 ounces each)
1 quart chicken broth

1 Add the chicken to a medium pot. Add enough broth to cover by 1 inch. 2 Bring to a simmer and cook until the chicken is firm, about 15 minutes. 3 Let cool in the liquid for 5 minutes. 4 Drain and shred with a fork or slice. Ideally serve with tacos or on top of salads.

SAUTÉED

1 boneless, skinless chicken breast
(8 to 9 ounces)
Kosher salt and freshly ground black
pepper
2 tablespoons canola oil

1 Season the chicken on all sides with salt and pepper. 2 Heat the canola oil in a skillet over medium heat. When the oil starts to shimmer, add the chicken and cook until golden brown, 12 to 15 minutes total, flipping the chicken once halfway through the cooking time. 3 Let the chicken rest for 5 minutes before slicing.

#SPOON Tip To season chicken breasts, you want to use a three-finger pinch of kosher salt and sprinkle it from high above so you get even coverage. Follow with 2 to 3 turns of a pepper grinder.

Fallback Chicken Parm

BEST FOR <u>a weeknight dinner when you don't feel like using the oven.</u>

SERVES 4
ACTIVE TIME: 20 minutes
TOTAL TIME: 20 minutes
LEVEL: Easy

Chicken Parm is one of those things you either always see on restaurant menus or ate growing up. Now it's time to take the molten cheese and lightly breaded chicken into your own hands and make an easy chicken dinner.

3 tablespoons olive oil

⅓ cup panko bread crumbs

¼ cup grated Parmesan cheese

½ teaspoon dried oregano

1½ pounds thinly sliced chicken cutlets

Kosher salt and freshly ground black pepper

2 cups prepared marinara sauce (16 ounces)

1 cup shredded low-moisture mozzarella cheese

1. Heat 1 tablespoon of the olive oil in a large skillet over medium heat. Add the panko and cook, stirring, until the panko is golden, about 2 minutes. Transfer to a bowl and wipe the skillet clean with a paper towel. Stir the Parmesan and oregano into the panko.

2. Season the chicken with salt and pepper. Heat the remaining 2 tablespoons olive oil in the skillet over medium heat. When the oil starts to shimmer, cook the chicken in batches until browned, flipping once, about 2 minutes per side. Pour the marinara sauce over the chicken and bring to a simmer. Sprinkle with the mozzarella, cover, and cook until the cheese has melted. Remove the cover and sprinkle with the panko mixture.

A Veg-Heavy Chicken Dish

BEST FOR **when you don't want to do dishes.**

SERVES 3 OR 4
ACTIVE TIME: 25 minutes
TOTAL TIME: 25 minutes
LEVEL: Easy

Need a glorious dinner go-to that doesn't require washing every pot you own? Make this one-pan dish that combines chicken, zucchini, and bell pepper when you're looking for a little extra veg, too.

2 boneless, skinless chicken breasts (about 1¼ pounds), cut into 1-inch chunks

Kosher salt and freshly ground black pepper

¼ teaspoon garlic powder

3 tablespoons olive oil

8 medium white or cremini mushrooms (about 6 ounces), thickly sliced

1 small red onion, cut into ½-inch chunks

1 small red bell pepper, cut into ½-inch chunks

1 medium zucchini, cut into ½-inch chunks

1 tablespoon tomato paste

2 tablespoons red wine vinegar

½ cup chicken broth

1. Season the chicken all over with salt, black pepper, and the garlic powder. Heat 2 tablespoons of the olive oil in a large nonstick skillet over medium-high heat. When the oil is hot and starts to shimmer, add the chicken and cook, stirring often, until browned all over, about 4 minutes. Transfer the chicken to a plate.

2. Heat the remaining tablespoon oil in the skillet. Add the mushrooms and cook, tossing occasionally, until soft, 2 to 3 minutes. Add the onion, bell pepper, and zucchini and cook, tossing occasionally, until they just begin to wilt but still have some crunch, 3 to 4 minutes. Clear a space in the middle of the skillet and add the tomato paste; stir it for a minute to toast, then stir it into the vegetables. Return the chicken to the skillet and stir in the vinegar. Add the broth and simmer until the liquid reduces and glazes the vegetables, and the chicken is cooked through, about 2 minutes.

VINEGAR 101

Sounds gross, but vinegar has some serious cooking flavoring power.

RED WINE VINEGAR
Best for cooking, vinaigrettes, and hearty marinades.

WHITE WINE VINEGAR
Not necessarily interchangeable for red, but also good to cook with, especially with chicken or fish.

DISTILLED WHITE VINEGAR
The really sharp one used for poaching eggs and pickling.

APPLE CIDER VINEGAR
More recently famous as a diet fad, originally known as an epic addition to dressings and can be used in pickling.

Deconstructed Chicken Pot Pie

BEST FOR **when you just need a little comfort food.**

SERVES 3 OR 4
ACTIVE TIME: 25 minutes
TOTAL TIME: 25 minutes
LEVEL: Medium

Chicken pot pie doesn't have to come from the freezer aisle. Make this savory and filling recipe in one pan on the stove and revel in the fresh mushrooms and scallions.

3 tablespoons unsalted butter

2 boneless, skinless chicken breasts (about 1¼ pounds), cut into 1-inch chunks

Kosher salt and freshly ground black pepper

8 medium white or cremini mushrooms (about 6 ounces), thickly sliced

1 bunch scallions, chopped, white and green parts kept separate

1 tablespoon chopped fresh thyme leaves, or ½ teaspoon dried

3 tablespoons all-purpose flour

¾ cup chicken broth

½ cup heavy cream or half-and-half

1 cup frozen peas and carrots

1 lemon wedge

Biscuits, for serving

1. Melt 1 tablespoon of the butter in a medium skillet over medium heat. Season the chicken with salt and pepper. When the butter has melted, add the chicken and cook, stirring, until browned all over, about 2 minutes. Transfer the chicken to a plate.

2. Melt the remaining 2 tablespoons butter in the skillet. Add the mushrooms and scallion whites and cook until the mushrooms soften, 3 to 4 minutes. Sprinkle the thyme and flour over the vegetables and stir to coat. Cook for 1 minute to toast the flour a bit, then stir in the broth and cream. Bring to a simmer and add the peas and carrots.

3. Return the chicken and any juices from the plate to the skillet. Simmer until the peas and carrots are heated through and the chicken is fully cooked, about 3 minutes. Add the scallion greens and simmer for 1 minute to wilt them slightly. Finish with a squeeze of lemon juice. Serve with biscuits on top or on the side.

#SPOON TIP If you don't want to eat something this heavy all week, portion it into containers and freeze for up to 3 months. Just buy the lemon and biscuits as you need them (or ditch the bread if you want it even lighter). Before reheating, thaw overnight in the fridge.

Damn Good Buffalo Chicken Dip

BEST FOR when you care more about the food than the game.

SERVES 10 TO 12
ACTIVE TIME: 15 minutes
TOTAL TIME: 50 minutes (includes cooling time)
LEVEL: Easy

Being able to make your own buff chick dip is truly a next-level life skill. Use a rotisserie chicken and cream cheese to achieve that buffalo flavor you love. Be sure to pick up some carrot and celery sticks along with your favorite crackers, because it's all about balance (or, in this case, crunch).

1 cup sour cream

½ cup Buffalo-style hot sauce

⅓ cup finely crumbled blue cheese (about 2½ ounces)

2 tablespoons milk

2 (8-ounce) packages cream cheese, at room temperature

2 cups chopped rotisserie chicken (from about half a chicken; skin and bones removed)

1 medium carrot, finely chopped, plus carrot sticks, for serving

1 celery stalk, finely chopped, plus celery sticks, for serving

Crackers, for serving

1. Preheat the oven to 375°F.
2. Mash together the sour cream, hot sauce, blue cheese, milk, and cream cheese in a medium bowl with a fork until chunky and combined. Stir in the chicken.
3. Scoop the chicken mixture into an 8-inch square baking dish. Bake until warmed through and light brown around the edges, 25 to 30 minutes. Cool for 5 minutes.
4. Scatter the chopped carrot and celery on top. Serve with crackers and celery and carrot sticks for dipping.

The baking dish doesn't have to be square, it just needs to be big enough to hold about 6 cups.

Rotisserie Chicken Caesar Wrap

BEST FOR using up your rotisserie chicken, obviously.

SERVES 1
ACTIVE TIME: 10 minutes
TOTAL TIME: 10 minutes
LEVEL: Easy

Even though we know by now that your heart is in learning how to cook, sometimes you gotta cut corners. Enter: rotisserie chicken from the store. Try this simple number that strategically combines store-bought Caesar dressing, some fresh veggies, and a whole wheat wrap.

2 tablespoons creamy Caesar dressing

2 teaspoons fresh lemon juice

2 cups chopped romaine hearts

¾ cup chopped rotisserie chicken (skin and bones removed)

2 tablespoons grated Parmesan cheese

Kosher salt and freshly ground black pepper

1 (10-inch) whole wheat wrap

2 to 4 tablespoons grated carrot

1. Stir together the Caesar dressing and lemon juice in a medium bowl. Add the romaine, chicken, and cheese. Toss to coat and season lightly with salt and generously with pepper.

2. Lay the wrap flat on your work surface. Lay the carrot in a line in the middle, leaving about 2 inches on both sides. Pile the lettuce mixture on top. Fold the sides of the wrap in, then fold the bottom up and over the filling. Press the filling in as you roll to form a tight wrap. Cut the wrap in half crosswise with a serrated knife (that's the kind with ridges).

#SPOON TIP Make the wrap more pliable by wrapping it in a damp paper towel and microwaving it for 15 seconds.

Curry Chicken Salad

BEST FOR **eating straight out of the bowl.**

SERVES 2 TO 4
ACTIVE TIME: 10 minutes
TOTAL TIME: 25 minutes
LEVEL: Easy

Eating the same lunch day after day can get sad and provoke the midday slump. Avoid the lunch rut with this light, flavor-forward chicken salad. 'Cause chicken salad isn't just for family picnics, and it's way better with curry.

⅓ cup plain Greek yogurt

1 tablespoon fresh lemon juice

1 teaspoon yellow curry powder

1 teaspoon olive oil

Kosher salt and freshly ground black pepper

2 cups chopped rotisserie chicken (from about half a chicken; skin and bones removed)

½ cup shredded carrots

¼ cup finely chopped celery

2 scallions (green parts only), thinly sliced

Fresh greens, toast, or crackers, for serving

In a large bowl, whisk together the yogurt, lemon juice, curry powder, and olive oil. Season with salt and pepper. Stir in the chicken, carrots, celery, and scallions. Cover with plastic wrap and refrigerate for at least 15 minutes and up to 3 days to let the flavors develop. Serve on greens, between two pieces of toast, or with crackers.

flavor twists

HONEY MUSTARD–APPLE
Forget the curry and mix 1 tablespoon of honey and 1 tablespoon of mustard into the mayo. Add ¼ teaspoon poppy seeds and ¼ cup each chopped cored apples and grapes.

BARBECUE-BACON
Substitute BBQ sauce for the curry powder and add ¼ cup chopped cooked bacon.

SMOKY CHIPOTLE
Substitute the curry powder with 2 teaspoons adobo sauce from chipotles in adobo and 1 teaspoon each chopped chipotle and honey.

Asian Chicken Lettuce Wraps

BEST FOR <u>when you feel like playing with your food.</u>

SERVES 4
ACTIVE TIME: 15 minutes
TOTAL TIME: 15 minutes
LEVEL: Easy

Try your hand at impressing your friends (or yourself) with this sweet-and-spicy chicken dish. Place this savory chicken concoction in a large serving bowl and let everyone assemble their own lettuce wraps. Keep napkins close by.

Zest of 1 lime and 3 tablespoons fresh lime juice

2 tablespoons vegetable oil

2 tablespoons Thai sweet chili sauce

1 tablespoon soy sauce

2 teaspoons sesame oil

2 teaspoons sriracha, or to taste

3½ cups chopped rotisserie chicken (from 1 whole chicken; skin and bones removed)

1 cup shredded carrots

2 Persian cucumbers (the little ones), diced

Kosher salt

12 whole large Boston or Bibb lettuce leaves, washed and dried

1 cup fresh cilantro leaves

½ cup chopped roasted salted peanuts

Pickled ginger strips, for garnish (optional)

1. Whisk together the lime zest, lime juice, vegetable oil, chili sauce, soy sauce, sesame oil, and sriracha in a large bowl. Add the chicken, carrots, and cucumbers and toss well to coat with the dressing. Season with salt.

2. To serve, spoon the chicken mixture into the lettuce leaves. Sprinkle with the cilantro, peanuts, and pickled ginger, if you'd like. Serve immediately.

#SPOON TIP Can you use toasted sesame oil instead of sesame oil? Yes, but cooking can turn it bitter, so it's best for dressing or drizzling when your dish is done.

PASTA

IT'S OKAY, YOU CAN EAT IT

THE ULTIMATE GUIDE TO PAIRING NOODLES WITH SAUCE

At some point, humans turned their backs on pasta (and carbs in general) and spread the message that if you eat them, BOOM—cue the bloat and toss the spandex onesie. First off, wear the onesie, always. And two, take back your right to carbo-load—carbs equal energy to get shit done. However, not all pasta is meant to be smothered in red sauce, so read on and embrace a new world of sauce and pasta.

1. Thin, light noodles are great for brothy soups. Try ramen or angel hair, which will absorb the flavor of the broth they're cooked in. Don't want long, slurpy noodles? Try smaller pasta shapes like orzo, ditalini, or pastina (stars).

2. Short tube pastas like rigatoni, penne, and ziti are great for casseroles and stand up to being baked in the oven. Plus, their hollow centers hold lots of sauce.

3. Thin noodles like linguine and spaghetti are perfect for light sauces such as lemon butter, marinara, or carbonara.

4. Cheesy sauces beg for cozy places to hide their gooeyness. So for macaroni and cheese, try classic elbows, shells, or something slightly elevated, like cavatappi or cavatelli.

5. Filled pastas such as a ravioli, tortellini, manicotti, cannelloni, and agnolotti only need a simple sauce, like brown butter, since their centers are stuffed with meat, cheese, or vegetables.

6. Rich meat sauces need noodles with structure to hold it all together. Try pappardelle, lasagna, or tagliatelle for a stick-to-your-ribs meal such as Bolognese or hearty ragùs.

7. Going for an Asian-style noodle dish? Try soba noodles made out of hearty buckwheat flour, which can stand up to thick, flavorful sauces, like a peanut sauce, or a stir-fry. For a heartier meal, try udon, a thicker, chewier version of a ramen noodle.

8. Go with a funky shape such as farfalle, rotelle, orecchiette, or fusilli for highly flavorful sauces such as pesto or thick meat sauces. These pasta shapes will hold the sauce and deliver a delicious bite whether served with a hot sauce or as a cold salad.

FARFALLE
+ PESTO

SOBA
+
PEANUT SAUCE

ELBOW +
CHEESE SAUCE
(AKA MAC 'N' CHEESE)

PENNE +
TOMATO SAUCE

Penne alla Leftover Vodka

BEST FOR when you've sworn off drinking vodka.

SERVES 4 TO 6
ACTIVE TIME: 15 minutes
TOTAL TIME: 30 minutes
LEVEL: Easy

Don't have enough of the hard stuff for a vodka soda? Promised yourself you're never drinking again after last night? Same. Use up that leftover vodka for this stellar sauce.

Kosher salt and freshly ground black pepper

1 pound penne pasta

½ cup vodka

1 (24-ounce) jar marinara sauce

⅔ cup heavy cream

⅓ cup grated Parmesan cheese, plus more for serving

¼ cup fresh basil leaves, torn

1. Bring a large pot of salted water to a boil. Cook the pasta according to the package directions and drain, reserving ¼ cup of the pasta water. Return the pasta to the pot.

2. In a separate medium pot, bring the vodka to a boil over medium heat and cook until it has reduced by half, about 2 minutes. Add the marinara sauce and simmer, stirring occasionally, until the alcohol evaporates, about 10 minutes. Stir in the cream and simmer until the sauce thickens, about 3 minutes more.

3. Carefully pour the sauce into the pot with the pasta; stir in the Parmesan and reserved pasta water. Season with salt and pepper. Transfer to a serving bowl, garnish with the basil and more Parmesan, and serve immediately.

easy upgrade
Make this boozy classic a lil' healthier by tossing frozen peas or chopped spinach into the sauce. Let it cook until the frozen peas are cooked through.

Chicken and Pesto Pasta

BEST FOR when you want something other than red sauce, for once.

SERVES 4
ACTIVE TIME: 20 minutes
TOTAL TIME: 20 minutes
LEVEL: Easy

Pesto, the ideal sauce for when you want to feel like you're getting in more greens, but you still want pasta. Learn how to amp up your store-bought (or blender-made) pesto by combining it with the fresh veg and protein below. This makes four servings, so you can have it in the fridge to grab for the week or freeze it for later.

1 pound boneless, skinless chicken breasts, cut into ½-inch pieces

Kosher salt and freshly ground black pepper

2 tablespoons olive oil

8 ounces rotini or fusilli pasta

1 head broccoli, cut into small florets

1 cup frozen peas

⅓ cup heavy cream

½ cup prepared pesto

½ cup grated Parmesan cheese, plus more for serving

1. Season the chicken with salt and pepper. Heat the olive oil in a large pot over medium-high heat. When the oil starts to shimmer, add the chicken and cook, stirring occasionally, until browned and just cooked through, about 3 minutes. Transfer the chicken to a plate.

2. Add the pasta, 2½ cups of water, and ½ teaspoon of salt to the pot. Simmer, stirring frequently, until the pasta is cooked halfway, about 6 minutes. Add the broccoli, peas, and cream, then cover and cook, stirring occasionally, until the pasta is al dente and the broccoli is crisp-tender, 5 to 6 minutes. Return the chicken and any juices from the plate to the pot, cover, and cook until just heated through, about 1 minute.

3. Uncover and bring to a full boil. Stir to coat the pasta, then remove the pot from the heat, add the pesto and Parmesan, and stir well to combine. Serve with more cheese for sprinkling.

#SPOON Tip If you want to skip this whole poultry situation, swap in tofu or roasted chickpeas.

Scrappy Cream Cheese Pasta

BEST FOR when you refuse to go to the grocery store.

SERVES 4 TO 6
ACTIVE TIME: 5 minutes
TOTAL TIME: 20 minutes
LEVEL: Easy

There will be days in life when all you have is a box of penne and a brick of cream cheese in the fridge and you're exhausted. Fear not, friend. Life will go on, because we have the ultimate scrappy pasta recipe known to man. Or wo-man. And it's oh so good.

Kosher salt and freshly ground black pepper

1 pound penne pasta

½ cup cream cheese (4 ounces), at room temperature

1 teaspoon dried oregano, or 1 tablespoon chopped fresh oregano

¼ teaspoon garlic powder

¼ cup thinly sliced fresh basil (optional)

1. Bring a large pot of salted water to a boil. Cook the pasta according to the package directions and drain, reserving ½ cup of the pasta water. Transfer the pasta to a large bowl.

2. Add the reserved pasta water and cream cheese to the bowl and stir until the cream cheese melts into a smooth sauce. Season with salt and pepper and stir in the oregano and garlic powder. Top with the basil, if you have any, and serve immediately.

5 WAYS TO PERK UP PASTA

Boost your bowl of carbs with these add-ons you probably already have on hand.

FRESHEN UP
Have leftover parsley, basil, or mint? Chop up whatever fresh herbs you have in the fridge and sprinkle them on top of the pasta just before serving.

NICE SPICE
True fact: Spicy foods make you feel full longer, so add some heat to your pasta with red pepper flakes.

EMBRACE THE ZEST
Follow this pro move: Grate some lemon zest over your pasta for a fragrant finish.

GET CHEESY
Make any pasta even more satisfying with fresh, grated cheese. No need to stick to Parm or pecorino: try goat cheese, blue cheese, or anything else that will melt.

ADD SOME CRUNCH
Toast and season some bread crumbs in a dry skillet, then sprinkle them on top of your pasta for a great texture and toasty flavor.

Baby's First Lasagna

BEST FOR **when you miss Mom.**

SERVES 6
ACTIVE TIME: 30 minutes
TOTAL TIME: 1 hour 25 minutes
LEVEL: Easy

Some days you just need your mom's classic lasagna. Here's how to make it on your own: a superpower you'll be able to use in life whenever you need it.

2 teaspoons olive oil

4 ounces ground beef

4 ounces spicy Italian sausage (1 link), removed from the casing

1 (32-ounce) jar Italian tomato sauce

Kosher salt and freshly ground black pepper

16 ounces ricotta cheese

½ cup grated Parmesan cheese

⅓ cup fresh flat-leaf parsley leaves, chopped (optional)

1 large egg, beaten

12 no-boil lasagna noodles

16 ounces shredded mozzarella cheese

1. Preheat the oven to 375°F.
2. Heat the olive oil in a large pot over medium-high heat. Add the beef and sausage and cook, stirring with a spoon to break up the meat, until browned, about 4 minutes. Add the tomato sauce, bring to a boil, and reduce the heat to medium. Simmer, uncovered, until the sauce has thickened, about 10 minutes. Taste and season with salt and pepper.
3. Combine the ricotta, Parmesan, parsley, if you'd like, and egg in a bowl and season with salt and pepper.
4. Spread ¾ cup of the meat sauce over the bottom of a 9 by 13-inch baking dish. Arrange 4 noodles on top of the sauce and top with half the ricotta mixture, ¾ cup of meat sauce, and ⅔ cup of the mozzarella. Repeat this layering once. Finish the lasagna with the last 4 noodles and the remaining meat sauce. Sprinkle the remaining mozzarella over the top.
5. Bake until bubbling, about 30 minutes. Let the lasagna sit for 15 minutes before slicing and serving.

Instant Ramen for Adults

BEST FOR <u>making your instant noodles a little healthier.</u>

SERVES 1 OR 2
ACTIVE TIME: 8 minutes
TOTAL TIME: 8 minutes
LEVEL: Easy

Ease into jazzing up your instant noodles by experimenting with different veggie and broth combos. You really can't mess this one up, so go with your gut and have fun figuring it out.

1 (3-ounce) package instant ramen (any flavor), seasoning packet reserved

1 cup mixed frozen vegetables

1 teaspoon ground turmeric

Kosher salt

1 cup sliced cooked chicken breast

1. Bring 2 cups of water to a boil in a small pot over high heat. Reduce the heat to medium and add the ramen noodles, frozen veggies, turmeric, ½ teaspoon of the ramen seasoning, and ½ teaspoon salt; stir to combine. Return the water to a boil and cook until the veggies are crisp-tender with some bite, about 3 minutes.

2. Add the chicken and cook until just warmed through, about 1 minute. Remove from the heat and ladle the vegetables, chicken, and noodles into a bowl. Pour the broth over the top and serve.

#SPOON TIP For a lighter-tasting broth, you can ditch the seasoning packet and use chicken broth instead of water if you dig more natural flavors or want to cut back on sodium.

Toasted Ramen Avocado Slaw

BEST FOR **using up that bulk pack of instant ramen.**

SERVES 4 TO 6
PREP TIME: 20 minutes
TOTAL TIME: 20 minutes
LEVEL: Easy

This noodle and veggie love child is definitely more salad than carbs, but that's totally okay with us. Embrace the added crunch because it's exactly what you need when you're starting to think you're overeating leaves.

1 (3-ounce) package of instant ramen, seasoning packet discarded

2 tablespoons unsalted butter, melted

⅓ cup vegetable oil

⅓ cup unseasoned rice wine vinegar

¼ cup honey

1 tablespoon soy sauce

1 teaspoon sesame oil (see SpoonTip, page 45)

Freshly ground black pepper

1 (12-ounce) bag coleslaw mix

1 avocado, peeled and cubed

1 cup shelled edamame, cooked

1 Granny Smith apple, peeled, cored, and cubed

1 cup roasted salted cashews, chopped

3 scallions, thinly sliced crosswise into 3-inch pieces

1. Preheat the oven to 400°F.
2. Crush the ramen with your hands into medium pieces and arrange them in a single layer on a baking sheet. Pour the butter on top and toss to coat. Toast the ramen in the oven until golden, about 8 minutes. Remove from the oven and let cool.
3. Whisk together the vegetable oil, vinegar, honey, soy sauce, sesame oil, and 1 teaspoon pepper in a large bowl. Add the coleslaw mix, toasted ramen, avocado, edamame, apple, and cashews. Toss to combine. Serve in bowls, topped with the scallions.

easy upgrade

Add shredded rotisserie chicken to get your protein on, or turn it into something a little bougier by topping with thinly sliced steak.

Beef Chili Ramen

BEST FOR when you're freezing and you don't control the heat in your apartment.

SERVES 4 TO 6
ACTIVE TIME: 30 minutes
TOTAL TIME: 30 minutes
LEVEL: Easy

A truly inventive take on your feel-good chili ingredients of peppers, tomato, beans, and ground beef, but with the addition of easy-to-make noodles. This recipe makes a lot of servings, too, so you can feed your roommates or store it in your freezer for later.

1 tablespoon vegetable oil

1 pound ground beef

1 small onion, chopped

1 small red bell pepper, chopped

3 garlic cloves, finely chopped

3 tablespoons chili powder

1 cup lager-style beer

1 (15-ounce) can tomato sauce

1 (14.5-ounce) can diced fire-roasted tomatoes

1 (15.5-ounce) can pinto beans, drained and rinsed

Kosher salt

3 (3-ounce) packages beef-flavored instant ramen, 1 seasoning packet reserved

Sour cream and shredded Cheddar cheese, for serving

1. Heat the vegetable oil over medium-high in a medium pot. Add the beef and cook, breaking up the meat with a spoon as it cooks, until browned all over, about 4 minutes. Add the onion, bell pepper, and garlic and cook until slightly softened, 4 minutes. Sprinkle with the chili powder and stir to coat. Add the beer and cook until the liquid has evaporated, about 2 minutes.

2. Add the tomato sauce, diced tomatoes, beans, and 3 cups of water. Simmer until slightly reduced but still soupy, about 15 minutes. Season with salt.

3. Add the ramen, pressing down to submerge it in the sauce, then sprinkle in one of the seasoning packets. Simmer until the ramen is just tender. (It should still have some bite, since it will continue to cook after being removed from the heat.) Serve immediately in bowls, topped with sour cream and cheese.

Literal Pasta Salad

BEST FOR when you just washed all your to-go containers.

SERVES 4 TO 6
ACTIVE TIME: 30 minutes
TOTAL TIME: 30 minutes
LEVEL: Easy

This underrated hybrid is equal parts crunchy iceberg lettuce and hearty pasta. Plus, we added in your favorite veggies for a lighter and literal take on pasta salad.

Kosher salt and freshly ground black pepper

1 (9-ounce) package cheese tortellini

3 tablespoons red wine vinegar

½ teaspoon dried oregano

¼ teaspoon garlic powder

Pinch of sugar

⅓ cup olive oil

1 red bell pepper, chopped

1 cup grape or cherry tomatoes, halved

8 ounces fresh mozzarella cheese, cubed

1 cup marinated artichoke hearts, drained and chopped

½ cup sliced green olives with pimientos

2 ounces thick-sliced Italian salami, chopped

½ head iceberg lettuce or 2 romaine hearts, chopped (6 to 7 cups)

1. Bring a large pot of salted water to a boil. Add the tortellini and cook according to the package directions. Drain, rinse, and pat dry.

2. Whisk together the vinegar, oregano, garlic powder, sugar, ½ teaspoon salt, and several grinds of black pepper in a large serving bowl. Whisk in the olive oil. Add the cooked tortellini, bell pepper, tomatoes, mozzarella, artichokes, olives, salami, and lettuce. Toss to coat everything in the dressing and serve.

EMBRACE THE

FISH

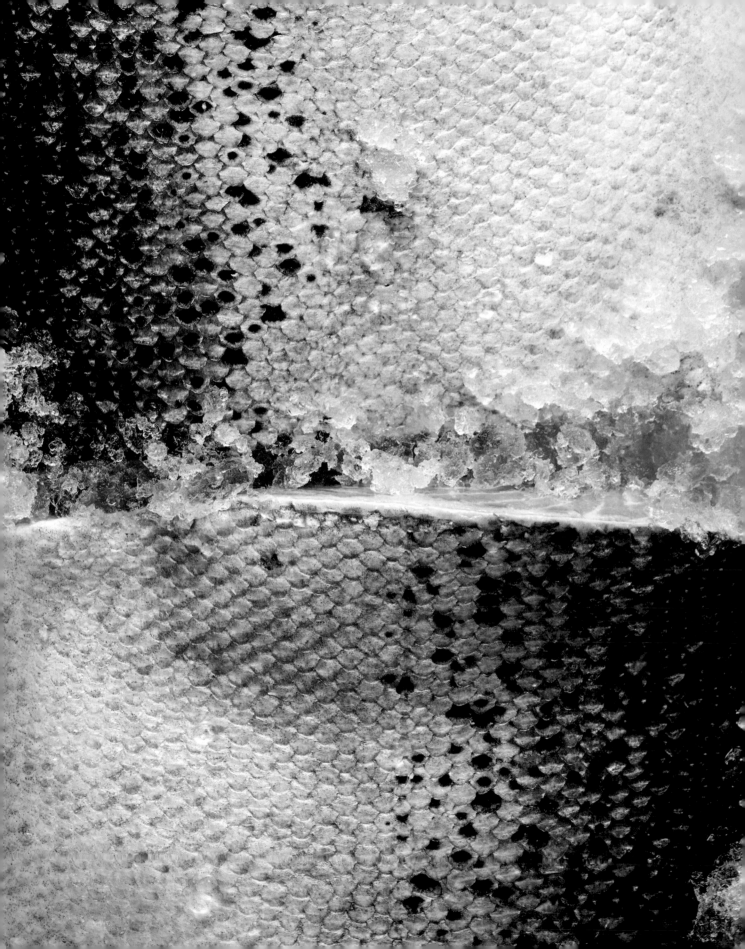

HOW TO MAKE SEAFOOD TASTE LESS FISHY

This is for the fish hater who is against fishy things. Ease into the seafood life by learning how to make your fish taste less like, well, fish. These are four simple marinades for two 6- to 8-ounce fillets of salmon (or any white fish) or 1 pound of shrimp that'll introduce new flavors and put the fish taste on the back burner.

SERVES 2
ACTIVE TIME: 10 minutes
TOTAL TIME: 1 hour 15 minutes
LEVEL: Easy

CURRY

2 tablespoons yogurt
2 tablespoons fresh orange juice
1 teaspoon curry powder

ITALIAN HERBS

2 tablespoons olive oil
2 teaspoons red wine vinegar
1 teaspoon Italian seasoning

TERIYAKI

2 tablespoons soy sauce
2 tablespoons light brown sugar
2 tablespoons unseasoned rice wine
   vinegar

DIJON

2 tablespoons Dijon mustard
2 tablespoons prepared horseradish
2 tablespoons fresh lemon juice

1. Combine all the ingredients for the marinade of your choice in a large zip-top bag. Add two 6- to 8-ounce fish fillets or 1 pound of shrimp, peeled and deveined, and seal the bag. Rub the bag to coat the fish with the marinade. Refrigerate for 30 minutes or up to 1 hour, gently shaking the bag once or twice to redistribute the marinade.

2. To cook, preheat the oven to 450°F. Remove the fish from the marinade and put it on a baking sheet. Discard the remaining marinade. Bake until the fish is just opaque in the middle, 4 to 5 minutes for every ½ inch of thickness or until the shrimp are cooked through, 6 to 8 minutes.

#SPOON TIP OF THE CENTURY: Don't be fooled: most shrimp sold at the supermarket fish counter are just frozen shrimp that have been thawed. That means the shrimp you find in the freezer aisle are essentially fresher than the "fresh" stuff.

A Comprehensive Salmon Dinner

BEST FOR <u>when you want to make dinner for your roomie.</u>

SERVES 4
ACTIVE TIME: 35 minutes
TOTAL TIME: 35 minutes
LEVEL: Easy

This recipe is one part stovetop and two parts oven. Cook the orzo on the stove while your lemon-and-pepper-crusted salmon and Brussels sprouts are roasting in the oven, and say hello to your new omega 3–rich diet.

1 pound Brussels sprouts, trimmed and halved

2 tablespoons olive oil

Kosher salt and freshly ground black pepper

2 garlic cloves, chopped

2 cups orzo

Zest and juice of 1 lemon

4 salmon fillets (about 6 ounces each)

4 ounces cream cheese

1. Preheat the oven to 450°F.
2. Put the Brussels sprouts on a rimmed baking sheet and toss with 1 tablespoon of olive oil, salt, and pepper. Roast until lightly golden, about 20 minutes.
3. While the Brussels sprouts are cooking, heat the remaining 1 tablespoon oil in a medium pot over medium heat. When the oil starts to shimmer, add the garlic and cook until lightly golden, about 1 minute. Stir in the orzo, 4 cups of water, and 1 teaspoon salt. When the water comes to a boil, reduce the heat to maintain a simmer. Cook, stirring occasionally, until the orzo is al dente, 10 to 12 minutes.
4. While the orzo cooks, sprinkle the fish with the lemon zest and season with salt and pepper. Remove the Brussels sprouts from the oven, push them to one side of the baking sheet, and place the salmon on the other side. Return to the oven and bake until the fish is just opaque in the middle, about 10 minutes.
5. Stir the lemon juice and cream cheese into the orzo and serve with the salmon and Brussels sprouts.

#SPOON Tip If you're freaked out by the gray flesh near the scaly part of the salmon, slide your spatula between the skin and meat when you take the pieces off the baking sheet and leave it behind.

Feisty Fish Tacos

BEST FOR dinner when you don't want another chicken breast.

MAKES 8 TACOS
ACTIVE TIME: 25 minutes
TOTAL TIME: 25 minutes
LEVEL: Easy

Figuring out how to make the items you always order at a restaurant is a special kind of win. But also, this simple and savvy fish taco recipe is ideal, 'cause it's mostly just assembling. Score.

Juice of 2 limes, plus wedges for serving

1 teaspoon chili powder

Kosher salt and freshly ground black pepper

1 pound tilapia fillets, cut into 2-inch pieces

1 (14-ounce) bag coleslaw mix

¼ cup mayonnaise

1 teaspoon hot sauce, plus more for serving

8 small corn tortillas

1. Preheat the oven to 425°F. Line a baking sheet with parchment paper or aluminum foil.

2. Mix the juice of 1 lime, the chili powder, 1 teaspoon salt, and a few grinds of pepper in a medium bowl. Toss the tilapia with the lime mixture, then transfer to the prepared baking sheet and bake until the fish is flaky and white on the inside, 10 to 12 minutes.

3. Meanwhile, toss the coleslaw mix, remaining lime juice, mayonnaise, hot sauce, and ½ teaspoon salt in a medium bowl until the coleslaw mix is coated. Warm the tortillas according to the package directions. Assemble the tacos with the tilapia and cabbage. Serve with lime wedges and hot sauce.

Loaded Shrimp Nachos

BEST FOR <u>5 p.m. on Saturdays when you've given up on finding the energy to go out.</u>

SERVES 4
ACTIVE TIME: 20 minutes
TOTAL TIME: 20 minutes
LEVEL: Easy

Cheese. Chips. Shrimp. Jalapeños. Sour cream magic. It's the stuff of legends. 'Nuff said.

1 tablespoon olive oil

1 pound small shrimp, peeled and deveined, tails removed

Kosher salt and freshly ground black pepper

1 tablespoon taco seasoning

½ cup sour cream, plus more for topping

½ cup salsa, plus more for topping

1 (9-ounce) bag corn tortilla chips

4 cups grated Mexican blend cheese

4 scallions, sliced

¼ cup sliced pickled jalapeños

1. Heat the olive oil in a nonstick skillet over medium heat. Sprinkle the shrimp with salt, pepper, and taco seasoning. Add the shrimp to the pan and cook, stirring, until opaque white inside and pink outside, 4 to 5 minutes.

2. Preheat the broiler. Transfer the shrimp to a bowl and mix in the sour cream and salsa. On a parchment paper- or foil-lined baking sheet, layer the tortilla chips and shrimp mixture, then sprinkle with the cheese. Broil until the cheese has melted, about 2 minutes. Top with the scallions, pickled jalapeños, salsa, and sour cream.

HOW TO ACTUALLY COOK SHRIMP

We'll be right back to our usual programming of exceptionally helpful and badass recipes after this brief message. It's time to learn how to cook shrimp.

BOILED SHRIMP

1 Add seasonings, like Old Bay or simply bay leaves and lemons, to a large pot of boiling water. **2** Add the shrimp (shells on or off) and cook until the shrimp are opaque white inside and pink outside, about 3 minutes. **3** Transfer to a bowl of ice and cold water to stop the cooking.

ROASTED SHRIMP

1 Toss peeled shrimp with olive oil, salt, and pepper in a large bowl. **2** Spread them out in an even layer on a large baking sheet. **3** Roast at 400°F for 8 to 10 minutes, until the shrimp are opaque white inside and pink outside. And *boom*. That's it.

SAUTÉED SHRIMP

1 Heat a few tablespoons of olive oil in a skillet over medium-high heat. Add chopped garlic, cook for 1 minute, then add peeled shrimp and season with salt and pepper. **2** Cook until the shrimp start to curl and turn pink, about 1 minute. **3** Flip and cook until the shrimp are opaque white inside and pink outside, another 2 to 3 minutes, depending on their size. **4** Remove from the heat, then sprinkle with chopped fresh herbs and a squeeze of lemon. SO FRIGGIN' FAST!

Weeknight Shrimp Curry

BEST FOR when you discovered that random bag of rice in the cabinet.

SERVES 4
ACTIVE TIME: 20 minutes
TOTAL TIME: 20 minutes
LEVEL: Easy

This coconut milk–based curry is the only curry you'll ever need, and it just happens to be completely dairy-free. With a soft bed of rice and a bit of a kick thanks to canned chiles, it's a cozy dinner done right.

1 tablespoon vegetable oil

½ yellow onion, diced

1 garlic clove, grated

1 (1-inch) piece fresh ginger, peeled and grated

1½ teaspoons curry powder

Kosher salt and freshly ground black pepper

1 (10-ounce) can diced tomatoes with green chiles

1 (13.5-ounce) can coconut milk

1 pound medium shrimp, peeled and deveined, tails removed, if desired

Cooked rice, for serving

Lime wedges, for serving (optional)

1. Heat the vegetable oil in a large skillet over medium-high heat. When the oil starts to shimmer, stir in the onion, garlic, and ginger and cook, stirring often, until the onion has softened, about 5 minutes. Sprinkle in the curry, 1 teaspoon salt, and several grinds of pepper, and cook, stirring, until the onion is well coated, about 2 minutes.

2. Add the tomatoes, using the back of a spoon to break up any large chunks. Cook until about half the tomato juice has evaporated, 4 to 5 minutes.

3. Stir in the coconut milk and shrimp and bring to a simmer. Cook, stirring often, until the shrimp are pink and opaque throughout, about 5 minutes. Serve with rice and lime wedges, if you'd like.

Your Basic Tuna Salad

SERVES 3 TO 4
ACTIVE TIME: 15 minutes
TOTAL TIME: 15 minutes
LEVEL: Easy

Embrace the tuna salad, and you'll never go back to plain turkey sandwiches. A word to the wise: Don't break out your tuna sandwich in a confined spaced or on an airplane.

¼ small red onion, finely chopped

2 (6-ounce) cans white meat tuna packed in water, drained

¾ cup mayonnaise

1 teaspoon Dijon mustard

1 small celery stalk, finely chopped

Freshly ground black pepper

1. Soak the onion in cold water for 5 minutes to mellow its bite; drain.
2. Break up the tuna with a fork in a bowl. Add the drained onion, mayonnaise, mustard, and celery; stir to combine. Season with pepper.

easy upgrade

Make your canned fish lunch sexier by adding fresh lemon juice, or for a sweet and savory vibe, toss in some dried cranberries.

Tuna Pasta Salad 2.0

BEST FOR when you're relying on your pantry for sustenance.

SERVES 4 TO 6
ACTIVE TIME: 20 minutes
TOTAL TIME: 1 hour 20 minutes
(includes chilling time)
LEVEL: Easy

Canned tuna is basically the most affordable seafood you can buy (plus, you can usually find it at your local convenience store). Toss it with rigatoni pasta and a few healthy mix-ins for a budget-friendly meal that seriously hits the spot.

Kosher salt and freshly ground black pepper

1 pound rigatoni

2 (6-ounce) cans white meat tuna packed in water, drained

2 cups baby spinach

1 pint cherry tomatoes, halved

2 celery stalks, sliced into ¼-inch pieces

¼ small red onion, diced

¼ cup white wine vinegar

¼ cup olive oil

8 ounces sharp Cheddar cheese, cut into ½-inch cubes

1. Bring a large pot of salted water to a boil. Cook the pasta according to the package directions until al dente. Drain and rinse with cold water; set aside.

2. Mix the tuna, spinach, tomatoes, celery, onion, vinegar, olive oil, 2 teaspoons salt, and pepper to taste in a large bowl. Add the pasta and Cheddar and toss until well coated. Refrigerate until cold, about 1 hour. Serve cold.

Shrimp Scampi with Zoodles

BEST FOR <u>first-time spiralizers.</u>

SERVES 4
ACTIVE TIME: 20 minutes
TOTAL TIME: 20 minutes
LEVEL: Easy

The words "scampi" and "zoodles" might sound out of this world, but the sooner you ground yourself in this super-simple veggie take on shrimp scampi, the sooner you'll find some much needed balance to your busy week. Meaning, you'll get your veg and some lean protein all in one swoop. Plus, it's garlicky and gorgeous as hell and we love it.

8 tablespoons (1 stick) unsalted butter, cut into cubes

3 or 4 garlic cloves, minced

½ teaspoon red pepper flakes

Zest and juice of 1 lemon, plus wedges for serving

1 pound medium shrimp, peeled and deveined, tails removed, if desired

Kosher salt and freshly ground black pepper

6 cups (about 1 pound) zucchini noodles

¼ cup chopped fresh flat-leaf parsley

1. Melt the butter in a large skillet over medium-high heat. Add the garlic and red pepper flakes and cook, stirring, until fragrant, about 2 minutes. Add ½ cup of water, the lemon zest, and the lemon juice and cook until the liquid has reduced by half and thickened slightly, 4 to 5 minutes. Add the shrimp, ½ teaspoon of salt, and a few grinds of pepper and cook, stirring frequently, until the shrimp start to turn pink on the outside but are still translucent inside, about 3 minutes.

2. Add the zucchini noodles and toss until they are coated with the sauce and have wilted slightly, about 3 minutes. Sprinkle in the parsley, season with salt and pepper, and serve with lemon wedges.

#SPOON TIP Zoodles can easily be made with a spiralizer machine, vegetable peeler, or box grater. Pre-spiralized zoodles are sold at many grocery stores.

MASH POTATOES LIKE A BOSS

The easiest way to start experimenting with potatoes is to mash 'em. Here's how you can have your favorite comfort food when you are feeling healthy, are in a hurry, or want potatoes with something other than butter.

SERVES 4
ACTIVE TIME: 20 minutes
TOTAL TIME: 30 minutes
LEVEL: Easy

2 pounds russet potatoes (about 4 medium), peeled

Kosher salt and freshly ground black pepper

¾ cup whole milk

4 to 8 tablespoons (½ to 1 stick) unsalted butter

1. Cut potatoes into 1-inch cubes and place them in a large pot. Add 1 teaspoon salt and cold water to cover by about 3 inches.
2. Bring the water to a boil over high heat. Reduce the heat to maintain a simmer and cook until a fork goes into the potatoes easily, about 10 minutes.
3. Drain the potatoes and mash them in the pot with a potato masher or a fork.
4. Meanwhile, put the milk and butter in a microwave-safe bowl and microwave until the butter has just melted, about 1 minute. Add the mixture to the potatoes and continue mashing until most of the lumps are gone and the texture is light and airy. Don't mash them to death, though—they'll get gluey.
5. Season with 1½ teaspoons salt and pepper to taste.

~~~ **variations** ~~~

OLIVE OIL POTATOES
Substitute ⅔ cup extra-virgin olive oil for the milk and butter. Mix in 3 chopped scallions and the juice of 1 lemon. Top with chopped scallions.

COCONUT SWEET POTATOES
Substitute sweet potatoes for the russets. Substitute coconut oil for the butter.

BACON SOUR CREAM POTATOES
1. Cook 4 slices of bacon in a skillet over medium heat until crispy, about 3 minutes per side. Drain the bacon on a paper towel–lined plate and reserve 1 tablespoon of the bacon fat.
2. Substitute the reserved bacon fat for the butter and 1 cup of heavy cream for the milk.
3. Add ½ cup sour cream and mash the potatoes until smooth and creamy.
4. Crumble the bacon and mix half into the potatoes.
5. Top the potatoes with a dollop of sour cream and the remaining bacon crumbles.

OLIVE OIL POTATOES

BACON SOUR
CREAM POTATOES

COCONUT SWEET
POTATOES

CLASSIC MASHED
POTATOES

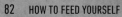

ALL THE WAYS TO COOK POTATOES

MICROWAVE

1 large russet or sweet potato,
  scrubbed

1 Prick the potato all over with a
fork. 2 Wrap in a damp paper
towel and microwave until tender,
flipping to the other side halfway
through, about 7 minutes for
russet potato and 6 minutes for
sweet potato. 3 Wrap the hot
potato in aluminum foil and let
stand for 2 minutes.

TOASTER OVEN

4 russet or sweet potatoes,
  scrubbed
Olive oil
Kosher salt

1 Preheat a toaster oven to
400ºF. 2 Prick the potatoes all
over with a fork. 3 Brush with
olive oil and sprinkle with salt.
4 Bake until the potatoes are
tender when squeezed, 1 hour to
1 hour 20 minutes.

STOVETOP

2 to 4 russet or sweet potatoes,
  scrubbed
Kosher salt

1 Place the potatoes in a large
pot. Add enough water to cover the
potatoes by 2 inches, then season
generously with salt. 2 Bring to a
boil and cook until a paring knife
easily pierces the center of a
potato, 40 to 55 minutes for russet
potatoes and 30 to 40 minutes for
sweet potatoes.

CONVENTIONAL OVEN

6 to 8 russet or sweet potatoes,
  scrubbed
Olive oil
Kosher salt

1 Preheat the oven to 400ºF.
2 Prick the potatoes all over with
a fork and arrange them on a
baking sheet lined with parchment
or foil. 3 Brush with olive oil and
sprinkle with salt. 4 Bake until
the potatoes are tender when
squeezed, 45 minutes to 1 hour.

SLOW COOKER

4 medium russet or sweet potatoes,
  scrubbed
Olive oil
Kosher salt

1 Prick the potatoes all over with
a fork. 2 Brush with olive oil and
sprinkle with salt. 3 Wrap in
aluminum foil and place in a slow
cooker. They should fit snugly
together; it's fine to stack them.
4 Cover (nope, no water!) and
cook on Low for 4 hours.

Healthier Loaded Sweet Potato

BEST FOR <u>when you're starting to make slightly healthier choices in your life, but you're still learning.</u>

SERVES 2
ACTIVE TIME: 10 minutes
TOTAL TIME: 20 minutes
LEVEL: Easy

This loaded sweet potato is all about giving your body things that make you feel good, like black beans and avocado. It'll also keep you full for the day ahead, whether you're running around like crazy or need to focus.

2 medium sweet potatoes

1 (15-ounce) can black beans, drained and rinsed

¼ cup of your favorite salsa

Kosher salt

1 small avocado, pitted, peeled, and diced

2 tablespoons shredded Cheddar cheese

2 tablespoons plain Greek yogurt

1. Wrap the sweet potatoes in damp paper towels and microwave until tender, 8 to 10 minutes, flipping halfway through.

2. Unwrap the sweet potatoes and transfer to a work surface. When cool enough to handle, slice them open lengthwise. Using a spoon, scoop out the flesh, leaving an ⅛-inch border on the skins; transfer the flesh to a bowl. Combine with half of the beans (reserve the rest for another use), the salsa, and a pinch of salt. Smash the mixture together with a fork.

3. Fill the potato skins with the potato-bean mixture and top each with avocado and 1 tablespoon each of the cheese and yogurt.

BBQ Chicken Sweet Potato Meets Avocado Whip

BEST FOR <u>a Sunday night dinner with the roommates, pre-5-hour TV marathon.</u>

SERVES 4
ACTIVE TIME: 30 minutes
TOTAL TIME: 40 minutes
LEVEL: Medium

Meet the sweet potato and chicken recipe of your dreams. These babies hold a ton of epic stuff, like avocado and cheese, and can be made six at a time in the oven.

AVOCADO WHIP:

1 ripe avocado, halved, pitted, and flesh scooped

1 tablespoon sour cream

1 teaspoon fresh lime juice

Kosher salt and freshly ground black pepper

POTATOES:

2 medium sweet potatoes

FILLING:

2 tablespoons olive oil

½ yellow onion, chopped

½ red bell pepper, thinly sliced

1 cup chopped rotisserie chicken breast (skin and bones removed)

Kosher salt

½ cup BBQ sauce

4 ounces Gouda, Cheddar, or Monterey Jack cheese, shredded

Fresh cilantro leaves, for serving (optional)

1. For the avocado whip: Using a fork, mash the avocado in a small bowl. Stir in the sour cream and lime juice. Season with salt and pepper and stir until smooth. Cover with plastic and refrigerate.
2. For the potatoes: Wrap the potatoes in damp paper towels and microwave until tender, 8 to 10 minutes, flipping once halfway through.
3. Unwrap the potatoes and transfer to a work surface.

When cool enough to handle, slice them in half lengthwise. Using a spoon, scoop out the flesh, leaving an ⅛-inch border on the skins. Transfer the flesh to a large bowl. Place the potato skins, boat-side up, on a baking sheet lined with foil.

4. For the filling: Heat the olive oil in a medium skillet over medium heat. When the oil starts to shimmer, add the onion and bell pepper and cook, stirring occasionally, until soft, 5 to 8 minutes, then transfer the vegetables to the bowl with the sweet potato flesh. Add the chicken and gently toss until just combined. Season with salt.
5. Spoon the filling into the potato skins. Drizzle the filling with the BBQ sauce and top with the cheese. Broil until the cheese is bubbling and golden brown, about 3 minutes.
6. Dollop each potato skin with the avocado whip, sprinkle with cilantro, if you'd like, and serve.

Potato Skins for the Win

BEST FOR <u>impressing your friends when they come over to watch the game or that reality TV show.</u>

SERVES 6
ACTIVE TIME: 20 minutes
TOTAL TIME: 1 hour 30 minutes
LEVEL: Easy

Learn how to make your favorite dinner app without having to pay more at a restaurant. Plus, these are great for when you're trying your hand at hosting and cramming people into your tiny apartment.

3 russet potatoes, scrubbed

8 tablespoons (1 stick) unsalted butter, melted

Kosher salt and freshly ground black pepper

½ cup shredded Cheddar cheese

Sour cream and chopped scallions, for serving

1. Preheat the oven to 350°F.
2. Pierce the potatoes all over with a fork. Bake directly on an oven rack until tender, about 1 hour. Let the potatoes cool.
3. Increase the oven temperature to 450°F. Quarter each potato lengthwise and scoop out the flesh. (Save the flesh for home fries or mashed potatoes—or eat it.) Brush the potato skin wedges with butter on both sides. Season with salt and pepper.
4. Bake skin-side up on a baking sheet lined with foil until crisp, about 15 minutes. Flip, sprinkle with the cheese, and bake until melted, about 3 minutes more. Top with sour cream and scallions.

#SPOON TIP If you're pretending to be sophisticated by hosting a party, bake the potatoes and prep the skins with the butter, then put them in the fridge. A half hour before your guests are supposed to arrive, set the skins out to take off the chill. Put them in the oven when people start to walk in the door, so they're hot and melty when everyone's ready to eat.

Buddha Bowl or Bust

BEST FOR a post-workout dinner for one.

SERVES 1
ACTIVE TIME: 15 minutes
TOTAL TIME: 45 minutes
LEVEL: Easy

You just kicked ass running that mile, lifting those weights, doing that yoga, and crushing that sweat life. Now it's time to refuel your body with healthy nutrients and proteins in this bowl. You'll feel healthy as hell and the right kind of full, we promise.

1 (15-ounce) can chickpeas

3 tablespoons olive oil, plus more for drizzling

1½ teaspoons garam masala, curry powder, or pumpkin pie spice

Kosher salt and freshly ground black pepper

1 large or 2 small sweet potatoes (11 to 13 ounces total)

4 large kale leaves, stemmed

¼ cup plain Greek yogurt

2 tablespoons smoked almonds, coarsely chopped

2 tablespoons pomegranate seeds

¼ ripe avocado, pitted, peeled, and sliced

1. Preheat the oven to 425°F. Line a baking sheet with aluminum foil.

2. Drain and rinse the chickpeas. Pat to dry. Combine the chickpeas, 2 tablespoons of the olive oil, the garam masala, and 1 teaspoon salt in a medium bowl, then spread them out on the prepared baking sheet. Bake until crispy and golden brown, 30 minutes.

3. Pierce the sweet potatoes all over with a fork. Wrap the potatoes in moist paper towels and microwave until tender, about 6 minutes, flipping once halfway through. Cut the potatoes down the center and scoop the flesh into a bowl. Season with ½ teaspoon salt and remaining tablespoon oil and mash with a fork.

4. Tear or chop the kale into bite-size pieces. Place in a microwave-safe bowl with 1 tablespoon of water; cover with plastic wrap and poke a few holes in the plastic to vent. Microwave until steamed and tender, about 3 minutes. Season with salt and drizzle with olive oil; toss to combine.

5. Mix the yogurt with 3 tablespoons water in a small bowl and season with salt and pepper to taste.

6. Place the mashed sweet potatoes in a serving bowl and top with horizontal lines of the kale, almonds, pomegranate seeds, chickpeas, and avocado. Drizzle with the yogurt sauce.

#SPOON TIP If you don't use all the roasted chickpeas in your bowl, save the leftovers in an airtight container to eat as a crunchy snack.

Badass Brown Butter Gnocchi

BEST FOR <u>when you want the "win" of making your own pasta.</u>

SERVES 4
ACTIVE TIME: 30 minutes
TOTAL TIME: 30 minutes
LEVEL: Medium

Just because you can't pronounce it doesn't mean you can't make it. This dish is as filling as pasta, but brings a little something extra to the table in the form pancetta (Italian bacon) and sage. If these lil' potato dumplings still seem intimidating, don't worry, we'll walk you through the whole thing. (P.S. It's pronounced: *KNOW-key.*)

Kosher salt and freshly ground black pepper

1 (15-ounce) can unsweetened mashed sweet potato, or 1¾ cups roasted and mashed sweet potato (no skin)

2 cups all-purpose flour, plus more for dusting

¾ cup cubed pancetta (6 ounces)

8 tablespoons (1 stick) unsalted butter

½ cup packed fresh sage leaves

Shredded Parmesan cheese, for serving

1. Bring a large pot of salted water to a boil.
2. In a large bowl, season the mashed sweet potato with 1 teaspoon of salt and ¼ teaspoon of black pepper. Slowly stir in the flour ½ cup at a time until the dough comes together in a ball. (The dough will be sticky). Dust your hands and work surface with flour and knead the dough a few times, then separate it into 6 equal pieces.
3. On a floured surface, using floured hands, roll each of the pieces of dough into a log ½ to 1 inch thick and 7 to 10 inches long. Add more flour if necessary to prevent the dough from sticking. Using a floured knife, cut the logs into 1- to 1½-inch-wide pieces.
4. Cook the gnocchi in two batches: Add half the gnocchi to the boiling water and stir with a wooden or slotted spoon to keep them from sticking. Boil the gnocchi until they float, about 2 minutes. Transfer the gnocchi with a slotted spoon or regular large spoon, tilting out the water, to a plate or bowl. Repeat with the remaining gnocchi.
5. While the second batch of gnocchi is cooking, cook the pancetta in a large skillet over medium heat until crispy and slightly browned, about 5 minutes. Transfer the pancetta with a slotted spoon to the plate with the cooked gnocchi.
6. Add the butter and sage to the skillet and cook over medium heat until the butter is golden brown and smells nutty, about 5 minutes. Add the gnocchi and pancetta to the skillet and toss to coat. Top with Parmesan and serve immediately.

THE GUIDE TO TOAST YOU NEVER KNEW YOU NEEDED

Running low on groceries? Enter: pizza toast. Need a dessert but don't have ingredients? Bring on the classic combo of cinnamon and sugar. Whenever you need a shoulder to cry on, toast will be there. Even if you don't have a hand-me-down toaster, or room on your counter for one, read below for how to get that soft bread toasted.

BROILER/OVEN

If you've already explored our egg chapter (pages 14–29), we've shared with you how to use your broiler and now it's time to use it as a toaster. **1** Place sliced bread, coated lightly with olive oil or butter, on foil (or a baking sheet). **2** Place on the top rack and broil for 2 to 3 minutes, flip, and toast for 1 minute more. This method will make the most toaster-like toast.

SMALL COUNTERTOP GRILL

Spread or spray olive oil on both sides of the bread, place it on the grill, and close the lid for 2 to 4 minutes.

PAN FRIED

1 Put a little olive oil or butter in a large skillet, place the bread in the skillet, and set a heat-safe plate on top of the bread. **2** Toast for 2 to 3 minutes on medium-high, flip, and toast for 1 minute more.

BE A GOOD TOAST PARENT

The number one way to take care of your slice babies is to pay attention to how you're storing them. This will prevent staleness and mold.

For bread you just bought, make sure you're locking in the moisture by keeping it twist-tied as tightly as possible. If your bread comes in a brown bag, wrap it up and place it in a plastic bag.

If you're trying to make your bread last longer than 5 to 7 days, you may want to consider sticking it in the freezer until you plan on eating it.

HONEY BUTTER
CINNAMON TOAST

CINNAMON-
SUGAR TOAST

ICE CREAM
SUNDAE
TOAST

PUMPKIN
CINNAMON TOAST

recipes on next page

Cinnamon Toast, 4 Ways

BEST FOR when you're craving dessert and you've run out of chocolate.

We created this cinnamon sugar recipe in just the right amount to fit in your average spice jar, so you have it on hand whenever a craving for cinnamon toast strikes. You're welcome—now embrace the power of this unbeatable duo.

Cinnamon Sugar

¼ cup sugar

½ teaspoon ground cinnamon

Put the cinnamon and sugar in a spice jar and stir or shake to combine.

#SPOON TIP If you don't feel like making a big batch of cinnamon sugar, you can always just eyeball it and sprinkle with a spoon.

CINNAMON-SUGAR TOAST

1. Toast 2 pieces of bread and spread with unsalted butter.
2. Sprinkle with cinnamon sugar.

HONEY BUTTER CINNAMON TOAST

1. Combine 8 tablespoons (1 stick) room-temperature unsalted butter with 2 tablespoons honey in a small bowl.
2. Toast 2 pieces of bread and spread generously with the honey butter.
3. Sprinkle with cinnamon-sugar and drizzle with honey. Save remaining butter for more toast.

PUMPKIN CINNAMON TOAST

1. Combine ¼ cup canned pumpkin puree with 1 tablespoon cinnamon sugar.
2. Toast 2 pieces of bread and spread with unsalted butter.
3. Spread the spiced pumpkin puree over each toast.

ICE CREAM SUNDAE TOAST

1. Toast 2 pieces of bread and spread with unsalted butter.
2. Sprinkle with cinnamon sugar.
3. Top with scoops of vanilla ice cream and mixed berries.
4. Drizzle with honey.

French Toast for Every Season

BEST FOR every Saturday for the rest of your life.

#SPOON TIP If you're making multiple batches for a big group, you can keep the finished toasts warm in the oven set to 200°F until you're ready to serve.

SERVES 4
ACTIVE TIME: 45 minutes
TOTAL TIME: 45 minutes
LEVEL: Medium

Making average French toast taste exceptional has everything to do with how fresh the ingredients are. That, and the amount of whipped cream involved. That's why we figured out the very best toppings for your French toast for every season, from fruit to dollops of whipped cream. Switch up your bread! Try challah for an extra-rich flavor or Texas toast for a thicker, heartier French toast.

8 large eggs

1½ cups half-and-half

3 tablespoons sugar

2 teaspoons vanilla extract

1½ teaspoons ground cinnamon

⅛ teaspoon kosher salt

8 slices potato bread

4 tablespoons (½ stick) unsalted butter, plus more for serving

Maple syrup, for serving

1. Whisk together the eggs, half-and-half, sugar, vanilla, cinnamon, and salt in a large bowl.

2. Heat a large nonstick skillet over medium heat. Soak 2 slices of the bread in the egg mixture, 15 seconds per side. Melt 1 tablespoon of the butter in the skillet and add the soaked bread. Cook until golden brown, about 2 minutes per side. Wipe out the skillet, add more butter, and repeat with the remaining bread, using 1 tablespoon butter for each batch.

3. Serve with maple syrup and butter.

～ seasonal variations ～

WINTER
[1] Combine 1 (16-ounce) bag frozen cranberries, the zest and juice of 1 orange, and ½ cup sugar in a pot. [2] Simmer over low heat until the cranberries break down and release their juices, 15 to 20 minutes. [3] Top your French toast with maple syrup and the cranberry compote.

SPRING
[1] Combine 2 cups fresh or frozen strawberries with 2 tablespoons water in a pot. [2] Simmer over low heat until the strawberries break down and release their juices, about 10 minutes. [3] Top your French toast with maple syrup, the strawberry compote, and a sprinkle of confectioners' sugar.

SUMMER
Top your French toast with thinly sliced ripe peaches and a dollop of whipped cream, along with a drizzle of maple syrup.

FALL
[1] Make your French toast but replace the cinnamon with 1½ teaspoons pumpkin pie spice. [2] Add 1 cup canned pumpkin puree to the egg mixture. [3] Top with maple syrup and ¼ cup toasted pepitas (pumpkin seeds).

A Seedy Toast You Can Trust

BEST FOR <u>when you want to feel healthy and fancy in the morning.</u>

SERVES 1
ACTIVE TIME: 5 minutes
TOTAL TIME: 5 minutes
LEVEL: Easy

If you have bags or jars of seeds lying around from when you went on that smoothie kick months ago, now you have a new reason to use them. Nut butter toast for all.

2 slices whole wheat bread, toasted

2 tablespoons creamy peanut butter

½ teaspoon chia seeds

½ teaspoon salted hulled sunflower seeds

Honey or agave nectar, for drizzling

Spread each piece of toast with 1 tablespoon of the peanut butter and sprinkle with ¼ teaspoon each of the chia seeds and the sunflower seeds. Drizzle with honey or agave.

DOUGH THAT MAKES US DANCE

Grab a different loaf this week and enjoy the wide world of store-bought bread.

EZEKIEL BREAD gets its street cred and style by using sprouted grains, which increase the number of good vitamins you're getting. Ya know, the ones you're probably not consuming during the weeks all you want are pizza or tacos.

OAT BREAD, especially the whole-grain kind, can be a richer source of carbs and protein opposed to regular white bread.

RYE BREAD is that friend you can call when you need more flavor in your life, or a heavier base for your toast toppings.

POTATO BREAD is spongier than your average loaf, which makes for a subtle but great swap for your turkey sandwich.

FRENCH BREAD, the only white bread worthy of this list, is best in the form of a skinny baguette and as a vehicle for cheese, meats, and some cool jams.

Mediterranean Toast

BEST FOR <u>people who hate salads.</u>

SERVES 1
ACTIVE TIME: 5 minutes
TOTAL TIME: 5 minutes
LEVEL: Easy

Inspired by classic Greek salad ingredients (tomato, cukes, and feta), this toast creation is the solve for when you're passing through your apartment for lunch but gotta keep moving.

2 tablespoons plain Greek yogurt

1 slice whole wheat bread, toasted

6 thin cucumber slices

3 cherry tomatoes, halved

3 pitted Kalamata olives, sliced

1 tablespoon crumbled feta cheese

Kosher salt and freshly ground black pepper

Olive oil, for drizzling

Spread the yogurt over the toast, then arrange the cucumber and tomatoes on top. Sprinkle with the olives and feta; season with salt and pepper. Drizzle with oil.

Desperate Times Pizza Toast

BEST FOR <u>late-night cravings when all the pizza places have closed.</u>

SERVES 1
ACTIVE TIME: 5 minutes
TOTAL TIME: 5 minutes
LEVEL: Easy

Scrappy? Yes. Tastes like pizza? Absolutely. Pro move: make a few toasts in a large skillet, then cut in squares for a crowd.

2 teaspoons olive oil

1 slice whole wheat bread

2 tablespoons marinara sauce

3 tablespoons shredded low-moisture mozzarella cheese

Torn fresh basil leaves, for garnish (optional)

1. Heat 1 teaspoon of the oil in a small skillet over medium-high heat. Add the bread and cook until the bottom turns golden brown, 1 to 2 minutes.

2. Flip the bread and reduce the heat to low. Top with the marinara and cheese.

3. Add the remaining teaspoon oil to the skillet. Cover and cook until the cheese has melted, 2 to 3 minutes. Garnish with basil, if you'd like.

No-Bread Sweet Potato Toast

GLUTEN-FREE

BEST FOR when you're gluten-free or cutting down on white bread.

SERVES 1
ACTIVE TIME: 15 minutes
TOTAL TIME: 15 minutes
LEVEL: Easy

Sometimes you don't want a ton of bread, but you need a vehicle for good-for-you and delicious stuff, like pesto. Meet sweet potato toast.

1 large sweet potato

Trim the ends of the sweet potato, then slice it lengthwise into ¼-inch-thick planks. Toast the slices until charred and crispy on the outside and easily pierced with a fork, 9 to 12 minutes. You can use a toaster—keep pushing the lever down until the slices are cooked—or a toaster oven set to High.

∿ toppings ∿

SWEET POTATO CASSEROLE TOAST
Let the sweet potato toast cool slightly, then spread with Marshmallow Fluff; sprinkle with gluten-free granola and brown sugar.

PESTO TOMATO TOAST
Spread the sweet potato toast with pesto and top with halved grape tomatoes and shaved Parmesan cheese.

HONEY BANANA PEANUT BUTTER TOAST
Spread the sweet potato toast with peanut butter. Top with sliced banana. Drizzle with honey and sprinkle with honey-roasted peanuts.

BROWN SUGAR MAPLE BACON TOAST
Crumble cooked bacon over the sweet potato toast and sprinkle with light brown sugar. Drizzle with maple syrup.

FETA ARUGULA AVO TOAST
Top the sweet potato toast with slices of avocado and arugula. Sprinkle crumbled feta on top. Drizzle with olive oil and squeeze a lemon wedge over the top.

BLACK BEAN TACO TOAST
Mash some canned black beans and spread them on the sweet potato toast. Top with diced avocado, a dollop of sour cream, a drizzle of fresh lime juice, and red pepper flakes to taste.

Big-Batch Bruschetta

BEST FOR friend groups who are always hungry and need a snack before dinner.

SERVES 8
ACTIVE TIME: 10 minutes
TOTAL TIME: 15 minutes
LEVEL: Easy

Here's how to look sophisticated when calling yourself an adult still feels like a stretch. Make this tomato mixture in a large serving bowl, toast some bread right before your friends come over, and lay it all out for the ultimate DIY bruschetta.

4 Roma (plum) tomatoes, diced

2 tablespoons olive oil, plus more for drizzling

Kosher salt and freshly ground black pepper

10 fresh basil leaves

1 baguette, cut into ¼-inch-thick slices

1 garlic clove

1. Preheat the broiler and line a baking sheet with aluminum foil.

2. Toss the tomatoes, olive oil, 1 tablespoon of salt, and pepper to taste in a medium bowl. Tear the basil leaves into small pieces and add them to the tomato mixture.

3. Arrange the baguette slices on the prepared baking sheet and drizzle with oil. Broil, flipping once, until toasted, about 2 minutes. Cut the end off the garlic clove and rub each slice of baguette with the cut side of the garlic clove. Serve the baguette alongside the tomato mixture.

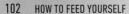

#SPOON TIP If your broiler's not working (or full of pans), toast the bread in a 350°F oven.

Non-basic Avocado Toast

BEST FOR when you want to turn avo toast from a breakfast into a legit brunch.

SERVES 1
ACTIVE TIME: 20 minutes
TOTAL TIME: 30 minutes
LEVEL: Easy

Don't roll your eyes at the words "avocado toast." We're simply just giving you another excuse in this book to eat bacon, cheese, and eggs. Again. Make these magnificent BLT toasties for your roomies on a Saturday morning, or just for yourself. And your hangover.

2 slices bacon

½ ripe avocado, pitted and peeled

1 teaspoon fresh lemon juice

⅛ teaspoon red pepper flakes

Kosher salt and freshly ground black pepper

1 slice whole wheat or crusty white bread

2 slices Roma (plum) tomato, about ½ inch thick

½ cup shredded pepper Jack cheese

1 large egg

1. Preheat the broiler and line a baking sheet with aluminum foil.
2. Cook the bacon in a medium nonstick skillet over medium heat until crisp, about 3 minutes per side. Transfer the bacon to a paper towel-lined plate and set aside. Remove all but 1 tablespoon of the bacon fat from the skillet.
3. Mash the avocado, lemon juice, and red pepper flakes in a small bowl with a fork until chunky. Season with salt and pepper.
4. Put the bread on the prepared baking sheet and toast under the broiler, flipping once, until golden brown, 1 to 2 minutes. Top the toast with the avocado mash, then the tomato and bacon. Sprinkle the cheese over the top and broil until it melts, about 2 minutes.
5. Meanwhile, heat the bacon fat in the skillet over medium-high heat. Crack in the egg, cover, and fry until the white is crisp at the edges but the yolk is still runny, about 2 minutes.
6. Top the toast with the fried egg.

HOW TO COOK ALL OF THE GRAINS

There are two main ways to cook grains, the pasta or pilaf method. We mainly use the latter, which means you add the grain to the water before turning on the heat. Meet nine grains that are waiting to rock your gluten-free or gluten-full world. Pair with sexy veggies or your fave protein.

WHITE RICE

When the panic about cooking rice all the way through sets in, just remember you need 2 parts liquid to 1 part rice. Bring to a boil, reduce the heat, and simmer, covered, for about 18 minutes. Remove from the heat and let sit, covered, for 10 minutes.

BROWN RICE

Follow the same rules as white rice, but let it simmer for 45 to 50 minutes.

FARRO

This grain can come regular, semi-pearled, or pearled, meaning the outer layer has been stripped off. Cook 1 cup grains to 2 cups water. Boil reg farro for about 40 minutes, 20 minutes for semi-pearled or pearled. Remove from the heat, drain if it's a bit soupy, and let sit, covered, for 10 minutes.

OATS

Move up in the world by not using instant oatmeal. Add 1 cup oatmeal to 1½ cups boiling water, then reduce the heat to low. Cover and cook for 10 minutes, stirring every few minutes, or up to 20 minutes for a creamier situation. Remove from the heat and let sit, covered, for 2 minutes.

QUINOA

Rinse your "keen-wah" before cooking. Add 1 cup grains to 1½ cups water, cover, and bring to a boil. The key is to reduce the heat and cook for 15 to 20 minutes. Remove from the heat and let sit, covered, for 10 minutes.

WILD RICE

Wild rice needs lots of water: 1 cup of grains to 2⅓ cups water. Bring to a boil, then reduce the heat to a low simmer, cover and cook for 45 minutes. Then remove from the heat and let sit, covered, for 10 minutes. Drain extra liquid.

BARLEY

Barley is thick and tastes kind of sweet. You can add it to soups, especially ones with hearty flavors. Rinse the barley and cook 1 cup grains to 1½ cups water, uncovered, at a bare simmer until tender, approximately 1 hour.

AMARANTH

These babies have a sesame-like flavor. To cook, use a ratio of 1 to 1, water and amaranth. Once boiling, cover, reduce the heat, and simmer until the water is gone, about 15 minutes. Remove from the heat and let it sit for 10 minutes.

MILLET

This grain is tiny and sort of tastes like a cashew. Rinse in cold water before using. The golden ratio is 3 cups of water to 1 cup of millet. Cover and cook for 15 minutes at a boil, then remove from the heat and let it sit, covered, for 10 minutes.

FARRO: THE MEATIEST GRAIN

WHITE RICE: YOU KNOW WHAT THIS IS

OATS: GOOD SOURCE OF FIBER AND CARBS

BROWN RICE: SOLID WHOLE-GRAIN OPTION

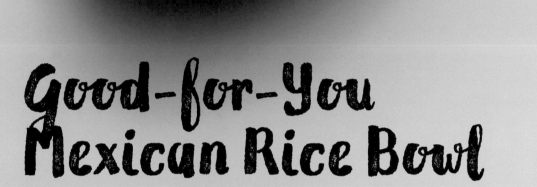

Good-for-You Mexican Rice Bowl

BEST FOR when you need dinner in under 15 minutes.

SERVES 1
ACTIVE TIME: 5 minutes
TOTAL TIME: 10 minutes
LEVEL: Easy

Make your leftover rice and random can of beans do more for you. With added avo and the option of Greek yogurt instead of sour cream, this take on beans and rice will fill you up and fit in any reasonable to-go container.

1 (15-ounce) can black or pinto beans, drained

½ cup leftover cooked white or brown rice

½ cup salsa

¼ cup shredded Cheddar or Mexican blend cheese, plus more for serving

1 scallion, sliced

Kosher salt

Sour cream or plain Greek yogurt, for serving

½ small avocado, pitted, peeled, and cut into cubes

In a microwave-safe bowl, combine the beans, rice, salsa, cheese, scallion, and a large pinch of salt. Cover with plastic wrap or a damp paper towel and microwave on high until the cheese has melted and the beans and rice are hot, about 3 minutes. Serve with a dollop of sour cream, the avocado, and more cheese.

BEC Oatmeal

BEST FOR those who think oatmeal isn't filling.

SERVES 1
ACTIVE TIME: 15 minutes
TOTAL TIME: 15 minutes
LEVEL: Easy

Not all bowls of oatmeal were made to be drenched in syrup and covered in brown sugar. Try this savory version of your go-to brekkie when you want more protein (hello, fried egg) and style (we see you, hot sauce).

1 slice thick-cut bacon

1 scallion, chopped

⅓ cup old-fashioned rolled oats

Kosher salt

1 large egg

2 tablespoons shredded Cheddar cheese

Hot sauce, for serving

1. Cook the bacon in a medium nonstick skillet over medium heat, flipping it once, until crisp, about 5 minutes. Transfer the bacon to a paper towel–lined plate, leaving the rendered fat in the pan. Let cool, then chop.

2. Add the scallion to the same skillet and cook it in the bacon fat over medium heat, stirring, until the whites just begin to soften, about 1 minute. Transfer the scallion to the plate with the bacon.

3. Put the oats, a pinch of salt, and ⅔ cup of water in a medium pot and cook over medium-high heat, stirring frequently, until the oats soften, about 5 minutes. Remove from the heat.

4. Return the bacon and scallions to the skillet and place over medium heat. Carefully crack an egg into the skillet, increase the heat to medium-high, and cook until the white is set but the yolk is still runny, 2 to 3 minutes.

5. Spoon the oats into a bowl and top with the bacon, egg, scallion, and cheese. Serve with hot sauce.

#SPOON TIP Have unflavored pouches of instant oatmeal? You can use those, too.

Taco Quinoa Salad

BEST FOR <u>when you don't want to be hungry after you eat a salad.</u>

SERVES 2
ACTIVE TIME: 15 minutes
TOTAL TIME: 30 minutes
LEVEL: Easy

This salad tastes like your favorite taco toppings—think lime and chili—but lives on a glorious bed of lettuce that is blanketed with spiced quinoa. Say hello to your new go-to dinner salad.

2 teaspoons tomato paste

1 teaspoon chili powder

¼ cup quinoa, rinsed

Kosher salt

2 tablespoons sour cream

Zest and juice of ½ lime

4 cups chopped iceberg lettuce

¼ cup shredded Cheddar cheese

2 tablespoons guacamole

2 tablespoons corn and black bean salsa, or your favorite salsa

2 large handfuls of corn tortilla chips, slightly crushed

1. Stir together the tomato paste, chili powder, and 1 cup water in a small pot. Add the quinoa and stir to combine. Bring to a boil, reduce the heat to medium-low, cover, and cook until tender, about 15 minutes. Season with salt and let cool for a few minutes.

2. Meanwhile, stir together the sour cream, lime zest, lime juice, 1 tablespoon water, and a large pinch of salt in a small bowl.

3. Divide the lettuce between two bowls. Top each bowl with half the quinoa, 2 tablespoons of the cheese, 1 tablespoon of the guacamole, and 1 tablespoon of the salsa. Drizzle with some of the sour cream-lime dressing. Arrange the tortilla chips around the edge of each salad and serve.

Mushroom-Quinoa Stuffed Peppers

BEST FOR when you want to fill up on veggies.

SERVES 4 TO 6
ACTIVE TIME: 30 minutes
TOTAL TIME: 1 hour 25 minutes
LEVEL: Medium

Challenge that gorgeous head of yours to memorize at least one filling-yet-nutrient-forward grain recipe. That way, you'll always have something healthy and satisfying to fall back on. If it were up to us, we'd choose these hearty, quinoa-filled peps.

¾ cup quinoa, rinsed

Kosher salt and freshly ground black pepper

2 tablespoons olive oil

1 small yellow onion, chopped

8 ounces sliced white mushrooms

2 garlic cloves, chopped

1 (15-ounce) can cannellini beans (or bean of choice), drained and rinsed

2 teaspoons Italian seasoning

1 (24-ounce) jar fire-roasted tomato sauce

3 red bell peppers

2 ounces feta cheese, crumbled (½ cup)

1. Preheat the oven to 375°F.

2. In a small pot, combine the quinoa, 1 cup of water, and ¼ teaspoon of salt. Bring to a rolling boil and then reduce the heat to maintain a low simmer. Cover and cook until the liquid has been absorbed and the quinoa is tender, about 15 minutes. Let stand, covered, for 5 minutes. Fluff with a fork.

3. Heat the olive oil in a large skillet over medium-high heat. When the oil starts to shimmer, add the onion and mushrooms and cook, stirring occasionally, until the onion is soft and translucent, about 7 minutes. Add the garlic and cook, stirring, until fragrant, about 30 seconds; remove from the heat. Stir in the cooked quinoa, beans, and Italian seasoning. Season with salt and black pepper.

4. Spread 1 cup of the tomato sauce in the bottom of a 9 by 13-inch baking dish or another dish large enough to hold the peppers and sauce. Halve each bell pepper and remove the seeds and core. Season the inside of the peppers with salt and black pepper. Stuff the pepper halves with the quinoa mixture and arrange them in the baking dish. Top the peppers with the remaining tomato sauce.

5. Cover loosely with foil and bake for 30 minutes. Remove the foil and bake until the peppers are tender, 15 to 20 minutes more. Sprinkle the feta over the stuffed peppers and serve.

Balsamic Chicken Sausage Grain Bowl

BEST FOR when you want to cook your own food, but with minimal effort.

SERVES 1
ACTIVE TIME: 15 minutes
TOTAL TIME: 20 minutes
LEVEL: Easy

This is the kind of dish that's technically made up of pantry and fridge staples, like chicken sausage, raisins, and almonds. But when you put it all together, it becomes a real meal, and you feel pretty good about yourself.

3 teaspoons olive oil

1 fully-cooked chicken sausage link, halved lengthwise and cut into ½-inch chunks

3 tablespoons roasted almonds, coarsely chopped

2 tablespoons raisins

1 teaspoon balsamic vinegar, plus more for serving

Kosher salt and freshly ground black pepper

1½ cups cooked farro or quinoa (from ¾ cup dry)

2 tablespoons grated Parmesan cheese

Chopped flat-leaf parsley, for serving (optional)

1. Heat 2 teaspoons of the olive oil in a medium skillet over medium-high heat until it shimmers. Add the sausage and cook until browned, 2 to 3 minutes. Add the almonds and raisins and cook, tossing occasionally, until warmed through, about 1 minute. Remove from the heat and stir in the vinegar and some salt and pepper.

2. Stir together the farro, 1 tablespoon of the Parmesan, and the remaining teaspoon oil in a serving bowl. Season with salt and pepper. Top with the sausage mixture. Drizzle with a little vinegar and sprinkle with the remaining tablespoon Parmesan and some parsley, if you'd like.

Easy Fried Rice

BEST FOR when you don't feel like paying for takeout.

SERVES 1
ACTIVE TIME: 20 minutes
TOTAL TIME: 20 minutes
LEVEL: Easy

Not only will this cost less, but it'll be far fresher and healthier, too. And if you're still wanting the fried rice flavor but in serious need of greens, up the amount of veggies you stir in and add less rice.

3 teaspoons vegetable oil

2 garlic cloves, smashed

2 scallions, thinly sliced, white and green parts kept separate

1 thick slice deli ham, diced

Pinch of sugar

1 cup leftover cooked brown or white rice

1 large egg

½ cup frozen stir-fry vegetables or frozen peas and carrots, thawed

2 tablespoons low-sodium soy sauce

1. Heat 2 teaspoons of the vegetable oil in a large nonstick skillet over medium-high heat. When the oil starts to shimmer, add the garlic, scallion whites, ham, and sugar; cook, stirring continuously, until the ham and garlic are golden, 2 to 3 minutes. Fish out the garlic and discard it.

2. Add the rice and cook, stirring, until heated through, 3 to 4 minutes. Push all the rice to one side of the skillet. Pour the remaining teaspoon oil onto the empty side of the skillet. Crack the egg into the oil, break the yolk, and stir until cooked through, about 1 minute. Mix everything together. Add the vegetables and soy sauce and stir until the vegetables are warmed through. Sprinkle with the scallion greens and serve.

#SPOON TIP Go rogue and add a squirt of sriracha for some extra spice.

Somewhat Wild Steak and Rice

BEST FOR <u>when your doctor says you need more iron in your diet.</u>

SERVES 2
ACTIVE TIME: 20 minutes
TOTAL TIME: 25 minutes
LEVEL: Easy

Choose this bad boy for the ranch pesto dressing and stick around for the good-for-you ingredients. Don't be wigged out about cooking steak for yourself: we all need go-to meals that keep us sated and loving life. *Sated* . . . what a bizarre word that we're also kind of obsessed with.

1 tablespoon ranch dressing

1 tablespoon prepared pesto

8 ounces flank or flat-iron steak

Kosher salt and freshly ground black pepper

1 tablespoon vegetable oil

1 cup frozen corn, thawed

1 cup cherry tomatoes, halved

3 cups cooked wild rice, warmed

1. Stir together the ranch and pesto in a small bowl, adding a few teaspoons of water to thin out the dressing.

2. Season the steak with salt and pepper. Heat the vegetable oil in a medium skillet over medium-high heat. Cook the steak until browned on the outside and medium-rare inside, 4 to 5 minutes per side. Transfer the steak to a cutting board to rest while you finish the dish.

3. Add the corn and tomatoes to the skillet, sprinkle with salt and pepper, and cook over medium-high heat, stirring occasionally, until warmed through, 2 to 3 minutes.

4. Cut the steak against the grain into thin slices. Divide the wild rice between two bowls; top each with corn, tomatoes, and steak slices and drizzle with some ranch pesto.

#SPOON TIP Make this meal prep even easier by picking up instant-rice packets at the grocery store. Any type of grain will work, too.

Hot Farro and Cheddar Side Dish

BEST FOR accompanying a chicken or fish dinner.

SERVES 4
ACTIVE TIME: 15 minutes
TOTAL TIME: 35 minutes
LEVEL: Easy

Farro is the meatiest, easiest-to-cook grain and goes great with any flavor combo. This comforting tomato-and-cheese version will make you feel accomplished, but in a cool way.

1½ cups farro

2 cups grape tomatoes, halved

1 tablespoon vegetable oil

A few dashes of Buffalo-style hot sauce, plus more for serving

Kosher salt and freshly ground black pepper

1 ounce extra-sharp Cheddar cheese

2 tablespoons grated Parmesan cheese, plus more for serving

1. Fill a pot with water and bring to a boil. Cook the farro according to the package directions. Drain and let cool to room temperature.

2. Meanwhile, preheat the broiler. Toss the tomatoes, vegetable oil, and hot sauce on a baking sheet and season with salt and pepper. Broil until the tomatoes are wrinkled and soft, 3 to 4 minutes.

3. Use a vegetable peeler to shave the Cheddar into thin pieces. In a large bowl, toss the cooled farro with the Parmesan and all but a few of the tomato and Cheddar pieces (reserve them for garnish). Season with salt, pepper, and more hot sauce. Transfer to a serving platter. Top with the reserved tomatoes and Cheddar, and sprinkle with more Parmesan.

#SPOON TIP Make an extra batch of the sweet oven-roasted tomatoes. These umami bombs are fantastic on burgers or with steaks as well.

THE 3 MOST BASIC WAYS TO COOK VEGGIES

We're not going to sell you on going vegan, and we'll only use the phrase "plant-based" once (that was it), but we *are* going to encourage you to embrace some of the most fibrous, unprocessed, good-for-you foods in the world. Specifically, we're gonna focus on one thing: WTF do you do to them to make them taste less like watery leaves? The answer lies within learning how to sauté, roast, and blanch, so you can master any veggie that comes your way. Frozen veggies are included here, too, because we believe in miracles.

SAUTÉ is fairly fast, if you're looking for that. The basic technique takes place in a skillet or pan on the stovetop. Use a little bit of fat (like oil or butter) and high heat to bring out the flavor of the veg.

ROAST is ideal when you have some time, are using hearty vegetables, or don't have room on the stovetop. This method will create a crunchier exterior, but will cook the inside as well.

BLANCH is the best way to enhance the natural flavor and color of vegetables. If you need to partially cook them to use later, aka meal prep because you'll be reheating them and they'll cook more, this is your method.

#SPOON TIP Always cut your veg so each piece is the same size—it's the key to even cooking, so some pieces aren't undercooked while others are mushy.

SAUTÉED

BLANCHED

ROASTED

SAUTÉ

Quick Guide. [1] Set a skillet over medium-high heat (that's a three-quarter turn of the dial) and add a drizzle of oil or a pat of butter.
[2] Swirl the pan around to coat the bottom. When the oil is shiny and starts to shimmer, or the butter has melted completely, add the vegetables.
[3] Season as you like . . . salt, pepper, spices, herb mixes, the works. [4] Stir to coat the vegetables in the fat until tender.

Commonly Used for Sautéing:

Spinach	3 minutes
Kale	5 minutes
Green Beans	5 minutes
Asparagus	5 minutes
Bell Peppers	7 minutes*

*the actual timing may vary, but you get the gist.

ROAST

Quick Guide: [1] Put all your vegetables on a baking sheet. Drizzle with oil. Season with whatever you like . . . salt and pepper are a good place to start, but experiment with spices and herbs. [2] Coat the vegetables in the oil and seasonings (the oil helps prevent foods from sticking and also encourages caramelization, aka the brown crispy bits that are the best part). [3] Stick the pan in a preheated 375°F oven and roast, tossing once, until you start to see those brown crispy bits and the vegetables are tender.

Commonly Used for Roasting:

Green Beans	20 minutes
Asparagus	15 minutes
Brussels Sprouts	30 minutes
Cauliflower	30 minutes
Carrots	20 minutes
Zucchini	15 minutes

BLANCH

Quick Guide. [1] Bring a pot of salted water to a boil (that means you flavored your water with a hefty pinch of salt). [2] Add your vegetables. When they are tender, drain and immediately plunge the vegetables into a large bowl of cold water with ice. This stops the cooking process immediately and retains the vegetable's bright color and fresh flavor. [3] Remove the veg from the ice bath and serve it cold, or finish it off with another cooking technique like sautéing.

Commonly Used for Blanching:

Broccoli	1½ minutes
Soybeans	2 minutes
Peas	1 minute
Brussels Sprouts	3 minutes
Carrots	2 minutes
Green Beans	2 minutes

OTHER WAYS TO MAKE VEGGIES TASTE GREAT

When you don't have the energy to legitimately cook but need the nutrients, dip 'em in these. The portions are a little larger so you can make them once and have them on hand all week when snack time hits.

HOMEMADE RANCH FOR YOUR NAKED VEGGIES

SERVES 8 TO 10
ACTIVE TIME: 5 minutes
TOTAL TIME: 5 minutes
LEVEL: Easy

½ cup mayonnaise

½ cup sour cream

⅓ cup low-fat buttermilk

2 teaspoons white wine vinegar

2 teaspoons dried chives

½ teaspoon dried dill

Large pinch of sugar (optional)

Large pinch of garlic powder

Kosher salt and freshly ground black pepper

Whisk together the mayonnaise, sour cream, buttermilk, and vinegar in a medium bowl. Stir in the chives, dill, sugar (if using), garlic powder, 1½ teaspoons salt, and ½ teaspoon pepper. Use as a dip, toss with a salad, or transfer to a jar or other airtight container and store in the fridge for up to 1 week.

BEET HUMMUS FROM SCRATCH

SERVES 6 TO 8
ACTIVE TIME: 10 minutes
TOTAL TIME: 1 hour 30 minutes
(includes cooling time)
LEVEL: Easy

2 medium beets, washed and tops removed (about 12 ounces)

1 small garlic clove

1 (15-ounce) can chickpeas, rinsed and drained

Juice of 1 small lemon

¼ cup olive oil, plus more for drizzling

3 tablespoons tahini

Kosher salt

Cover the beets in a medium pot with about an inch of water. Boil until a knife inserted in them slips out easily, 50 minutes to 1 hour. Drain and let cool. Peel and cut the beets into small chunks. Combine the beets, garlic, chickpeas, lemon juice, oil, tahini, and 1 teaspoon salt in a food processor. Pulse until smooth. Refrigerate in an airtight container for up to 5 days. Right before serving, drizzle with some olive oil and sprinkle with a pinch of salt.

Sorta Sweet Soy-Glazed Green Beans

BEST FOR when you need a side dish that rocks your world.

SERVES 4 TO 6
ACTIVE TIME: 20 minutes
TOTAL TIME: 20 minutes
LEVEL: Easy

Here's something green that's easy to make in a big batch. Transform your fresh green beans with this addictive soy glaze and sesame seed garnish, and you'll find yourself sneaking these out one by one every time you open the fridge.

3 tablespoons soy sauce

1 tablespoon toasted sesame oil

1 tablespoon unseasoned rice wine vinegar

1 teaspoon cornstarch

1/8 to 1/4 teaspoon red pepper flakes

2 tablespoons vegetable oil

4 garlic cloves, chopped

1 (2-inch) piece fresh ginger, peeled and grated

2 pounds green beans

Kosher salt

1 tablespoon sesame seeds, toasted

1. Whisk together the soy sauce, sesame oil, vinegar, cornstarch, and red pepper flakes in a small bowl.

2. Heat the vegetable oil over medium-high heat in a large nonstick skillet. Add the garlic and ginger and cook until the garlic starts turning golden, about 1 minute. Stir in 1½ cups of water and the green beans, bring to a boil, cover, and cook until the green beans are just tender, about 6 minutes.

3. Remove the lid and add the soy sauce mixture. Cook, tossing until the sauce thickens and coats the beans, about 5 minutes more. Season with salt, sprinkle with the sesame seeds, and serve.

#SPOONTip Don't be intimidated by fresh ginger! All you need for this recipe is a small piece. Use a spoon to scrape off the skin, then just grate it.

STIR-FRY: THE ULTIMATE VEHICLE FOR VEGGIES

BEST FOR every damn night of the week.

Here's your basic equation for a stir-fry you can rely on: Cook your protein in oil first, then set aside. Add aromatics, then veggies. When ready, add the sauce and cooked protein. Toss, garnish and you're a hero. Need the nitty-gritty? Look below for tips and tricks.

1. Have all your ingredients prepped and ready to go before you start cooking. Stir-fry is all about timing and quick-cooking over very high heat.
2. Cook in batches so you don't overcrowd the pan and end up steaming your meat and vegetables in their own juices. Always let the oil heat up before adding a new batch of ingredients.
3. Neutral oils (such as corn, vegetable, canola, and peanut) are used for sautéing, while flavorful oils (such as toasted sesame oil) should be used at the end.
4. Cut meat into bite-size pieces so it cooks quickly and evenly.
5. Chopped garlic, fresh ginger, and scallions are aromatics and will take no time to cook, so be mindful and have the next ingredients set to go. Also try chiles, herbs, chili pastes, lime leaf, and lemongrass.
6. Add firm or dense veggies to the pan first. Chopped carrots, onions, peppers, mushrooms, and broccoli need time and heat to soften and cook. End with the smallest and tenderest veggies, such as peas, spinach, corn, and grated carrots.
7. Stir-fries need constant stirring and attention: keep everything moving!
8. Add the sauce toward the end of cooking and toss so it thickens and coats the ingredients.
9. Garnishes can be almost anything that adds a new texture, including bean sprouts, peanuts, seaweed, crunchy sesame noodles, and fresh herbs.

CATEGORY

TERIYAKI

ITALIAN

SHRIMP SCAMPI

FAJITA

VEGETARIAN

LETTUCE WRAPS

BIBIMBAP

PROTEIN	AROMATICS	VEGGIES	SAUCE	GARNISHES
chicken (1 pound)	minced fresh ginger (2 teaspoons) minced garlic (2 teaspoons) chili paste (1 teaspoon)	broccoli (1 cup) red bell peppers (1 cup) snow peas (1 cup) carrots (1 cup) onion (½ cup)	terikayi sauce (½ cup)	sesame seeds scallions
Italian sausage (1 pound)	dried oregano (½ teaspoon) minced garlic (2 teaspoons) red pepper flakes (½ teaspoon)	red bell peppers (1 cup) broccolini (1 cup) zucchini (1 cup)	tomato sauce (½ cup)	basil Parmesan
shrimp (1 pound)	minced garlic (2 teaspoons) red pepper flakes (½ teaspoon)	asparagus (2 cups) cherry tomatoes (2 cups)	white wine (½ cup) butter (2 tablespoons) lemon juice (½ cup)	parsley
steak (1 pound)	minced garlic (2 teaspoons) ground cumin (½ teaspoon) chili powder (½ teaspoon) dried oregano (½ teaspoon) cayenne pepper (¼ teaspoon)	bell peppers (1 cup) onion (1 cup) tomatoes (1 cup)	salsa (¼ cup)	cilantro lime
tofu (½ pound)	minced fresh ginger (2 teaspoons) minced garlic (2 teaspoons) sesame oil (1½ teaspoons)	bok choy (1 cup) mushrooms (1 cup) baby corn (1 cup) carrots (1 cup)	soy sauce (¼ cup)	scallions sesame seeds
ground turkey (1 pound)	minced fresh ginger (2 teaspoons) minced garlic (2 teaspoons) chili paste (1 teaspoon)	bell peppers (1 cup) water chestnuts (1 cup) mushrooms (1 cup)	soy sauce (¼ cup)	lettuce leaves crispy fried noodles
beef (1 pound)	minced garlic (1½ teaspoons) sesame oil (1½ teaspoons)	carrots (1 cup) cabbage (1 cup) mushrooms (1 cup) bean sprouts (1 cup)	gochujang (Korean red chili paste) 2 tablespoons	kimchi fried egg

Roasted Zucchini Boats

BEST FOR __meatless Mondays.__

SERVES 4
ACTIVE TIME: 30 minutes
TOTAL TIME: 30 minutes
LEVEL: Medium

We give you zucchini boats, designed to carry whatever yummy or nutritious stuff you want in your body. We went with this cool artichoke, toast, and tomato ensemble, but feel free to make it more pizza-like with red sauce and more cheese.

4 medium zucchini

4 tablespoons olive oil

Kosher salt and freshly ground black pepper

1 cup crumbled feta cheese

1 cup grape tomatoes, quartered

1 teaspoon dried oregano

2 scallions, sliced

1 (14-ounce) can artichoke hearts, coarsely chopped

1 garlic clove, minced

¼ baguette, torn into small pieces (about 1 cup)

1. Preheat the oven to 450°F.
2. Halve each zucchini lengthwise. Scoop out the flesh, leaving a ¼-inch border; discard. If necessary, trim a small piece from the rounded bottom side of the zucchini so the zucchini sit flat, but be careful not to cut through the boat.
3. Brush the boats on all sides with 2 tablespoons of the olive oil and season with salt and pepper. Place them cut-side down on a baking sheet and bake until the zucchini is crisp-tender, about 10 minutes.
4. Meanwhile, combine the feta, tomatoes, oregano, scallions, artichokes, garlic, and baguette in a bowl. Season with salt and pepper.
5. Remove the zucchini from the oven. Using a spatula, flip the zucchini so the boat sides are up and fill each zucchini half with the artichoke mixture. Drizzle with the remaining 2 tablespoons oil and bake until the filling is warm and the top is golden brown in spots, about 10 minutes.

#SPOON TIP If the artichoke hearts aren't vibing with you, sub in broccoli florets or add halved olives.

Mac 'n' Cheese Meets Veggie Scraps

BEST FOR reducing food waste and making some comfort food at the same time.

SERVES 2
ACTIVE TIME: 10 minutes
TOTAL TIME: 10 minutes
LEVEL: Easy

Yes, this is a decadent mac 'n' cheese, and yes, it involves some veg. It's time to stop throwing away your broccoli stems and introduce them to the holy grail of feel-good foods. All your vegetable scraps are welcome to the cheese-carb party.

Kosher salt

7 ounces elbow macaroni (about 2 cups)

2 broccoli stems, peeled and cut into small pieces

4 ounces cream cheese

4 ounces mild Cheddar cheese, grated

½ cup milk

Additional vegetable scraps, such as chopped scallion tops, diced onion ends, chopped bell pepper scraps, grated carrot ends

1 heel of sandwich bread

A pat of butter

1. Bring a large pot of salted water to a boil. Cook the pasta according to the package directions, adding the broccoli stems to the water 2 minutes before the pasta is fully cooked. Drain and return the pasta and stems to the pot over medium-low heat. Stir in the cream cheese, Cheddar, milk, and vegetable scraps. Cook, stirring constantly, until the cheeses have melted.

2. Toast the bread until golden and spread with the butter. Tear into small pieces for bread crumbs. Divide the mac 'n' cheese between two bowls and top with the bread crumbs.

#SPOON TIP Use that boxed mac 'n' cheese you picked up on your way home. In the last 2 minutes of boiling the noodles, add the broccoli, then drain and stir in the powder.

10-Minute Vegetable Soup

BEST FOR **finally using those bags of frozen veggies.**

SERVES 2
ACTIVE TIME: 10 minutes
TOTAL TIME: 10 minutes
LEVEL: Easy

Chicken broth plus frozen vegetables equals sick-day goodness. It's not your grandma's recipe, but it still soothes the soul when your hustlin' self needs some TLC.

1 (32-ounce) carton chicken broth

1 (10-ounce) package or bag frozen mixed vegetables

1 cup frozen rice

2 handfuls of frozen leafy greens, such as kale or spinach

1 garlic clove, cut in half

Juice of ½ lemon

Combine the broth, mixed vegetables, rice, greens, and garlic in a medium pot and bring to a boil over medium-high heat. Reduce the heat to maintain a simmer and cook for 5 minutes. Remove from the heat and stir in the lemon juice.

#SPOON TIP More Flavor: Add nutmeg or ginger if you're looking for something warmer, or soy if you want toasty, salty vibes.

A Green Smoothie That Doesn't Taste Like Grass

BEST FOR when you're hungry but not hungry-hungry.

SERVES 1
ACTIVE TIME: 10 minutes
TOTAL TIME: 10 minutes
LEVEL: Easy

Get some more greens in your food by masking them with frozen fruit and other basic smoothie ingredients, like peanut butter. Sounds weird, but it's revolutionary, if you ask us. Happy blending!

1 cup frozen mango chunks

½ cup frozen kale

½ cup frozen spinach

½ banana

1 tablespoon creamy peanut butter

Put the mango, kale, spinach, banana, and peanut butter in a blender. Add enough water to just cover the ingredients (about 1 cup). Puree until smooth.

#Spoon Tip Starting with frozen fruits and vegetables means you won't have to add ice, which dilutes the flavor of your smoothie.

A Casual Kale Salad

BEST FOR when you want to feel fresh as hell.

SERVES 4
ACTIVE TIME: 20 minutes
TOTAL TIME: 20 minutes
LEVEL: Easy

Kale salad doesn't have to suck, thanks to our good friend citrus and partner-in-crime Parmesan. Plus, stock up on these simple dressing ingredients (white wine vinegar and honey mustard) so you can whip up this tangy dressing whenever you crave it.

1 bunch kale, stemmed, leaves chopped (about 8 cups)

2 oranges or 6 clementines

4 tablespoons olive oil

½ cup white wine vinegar

3 tablespoons honey mustard

Kosher salt and freshly ground black pepper

1 (15-ounce) can chickpeas, drained and rinsed

¼ cup shredded Parmesan cheese

¼ cup salted roasted sunflower seeds

1. Gently massage the kale by rubbing bunches of it together in your hands until you notice the leaves darkening slightly and becoming silky in texture. Toss the massaged kale with the juice of 1 orange or 3 clementines and 1 tablespoon of the olive oil in a large bowl until well combined. Let sit for 10 minutes.

2. Meanwhile, whisk the vinegar, mustard, ½ teaspoon of salt, and a few grinds of black pepper in a small bowl. Slowly drizzle in the remaining 3 tablespoons olive oil, whisking constantly, until well combined. (You can use a fork if you don't have a whisk.)

3. Peel and segment the remaining fruit. Add to the kale along with the chickpeas, cheese, sunflower seeds, and ¼ cup of the dressing. Toss until the salad is well coated. The remaining dressing will keep for 3 days in the refrigerator.

#SPOON TIP Take Massaging Seriously: Sounds weird, but this is the number one factor that separates people who love kale and those who believe it tastes like grass.

HOW TO TAKE CARE OF YOUR BANANAS

Nothing is as delicate as the life cycle of a bunch of bananas. One day they're green as hell, and the next day, mush city. That all changes today, when we take back control of our bananas. You can actually ripen bananas faster so they get on your page or turn the too-ripe-already fruits into some pretty fab recipes. Oh, you can also make stuff out of perfect bananas if you're blessed like that, including banana ice cream that's perfect for breakfast.

HOW TO RIPEN THEM FASTER

Place green bananas in a paper bag with an apple and store at room temp for 1 to 3 days. Check on your babies daily.

SLOW DOWN THE RIPENING PROCESS

You can try to delay the ripening situation by keeping the 'nanas at cooler temps, separating them, or covering the stems in plastic. However, nothing can stop mother nature from taking over, and the said methods are not always effective.

THE MADNESS BEHIND RIPENING

The reason why bananas turn so quickly (or take forever to turn yellow) is that the ripeness of the fruit is at the whim of a chemical reaction that happens when it comes in contact with ethylene gas. 'Nanas produce this gas naturally (the reason people believe you should cover the stem, so less gas is released), and the interaction breaks down the green stuff (chlorophyll) in bananas, making them softer, sweeter, and prepared for the spotlight in banana bread. If only Chem 101 was this fun.

#SPOON TIP If you're constantly overbuying bananas and can't eat them fast enough, take turns with your roomie buying them, so you can divide and conquer when they're at prime ripeness.

BANANA-BREAD
READY

WE'RE
NOT WORTHY

SO CLOSE
YET SO FAR

PATIENCE IS
A VIRTUE

WHAT EVEN
ARE YOU? A
CUCUMBER?

Straight-Up Banana Ice Cream

BEST FOR **when you need something sweet, but don't want to go too crazy.**

SERVES 1
ACTIVE TIME: 5 minutes
TOTAL TIME: 5 minutes (plus overnight freezing)
LEVEL: Easy

Obviously, this won't taste exactly like it would at your neighborhood ice cream shop, but it does the trick when you're out of store-bought stuff or trying to skip the extra sugar. Just remember to peel your bananas before freezing them, or you won't be having banana ice cream.

2 ripe bananas, peeled and sliced
1 tablespoon plus 1 teaspoon milk or flavored nondairy milk (such as vanilla soy or almond milk)

Freeze the bananas overnight until firm. When you're ready for ice cream, let the bananas thaw for 10 minutes. Pulse the bananas in a blender with the milk. When the mixture looks like sand, blend on medium-high until it reaches the consistency of ice cream. (Be sure to stop blending as soon as the ice cream becomes thick and creamy so it stays as cold as possible.)

want to mix things up? try these next-level variations.

GO FRUITY
Add ½ cup frozen fruit such as strawberries, blueberries, or mixed berries and 1½ additional teaspoons of milk.

GET YOUR CHOCOLATE FIX
Sub in chocolate syrup for the milk or add chocolate chips near the end of blending.

MAKE A MILK SHAKE
Add more milk for a drinkable version.

TOP IT ALL OFF
Drizzle with honey, or sprinkle with coconut flakes, or top with slivered almonds.

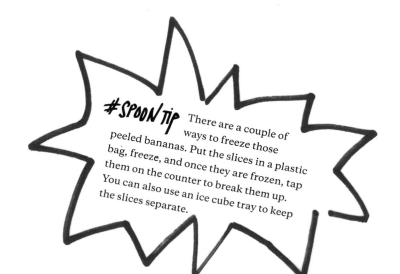

#SPOON TIP There are a couple of ways to freeze those peeled bananas. Put the slices in a plastic bag, freeze, and once they are frozen, tap them on the counter to break them up. You can also use an ice cube tray to keep the slices separate.

2-Ingredient Flourless Pancakes

BEST FOR <u>healthy weekend brunches.</u>

SERVES 1 OR 2
ACTIVE TIME: 10 minutes
TOTAL TIME: 10 minutes
LEVEL: Easy

It may take you a few tries to master this one, but have faith in mashed bananas. These banana pancakes are just the sexier version of plain flour pancakes and are totally worth it. If you're a 'nana pancake newbie, try the protein boost variation below, because the powder will make them easier to flip.

1 ripe banana

2 large eggs

Nonstick cooking spray

Maple syrup, sliced bananas, sliced strawberries, coconut flakes, and/or peanut butter, for serving (optional)

1. In a medium bowl, mash the bananas. Whisk in the eggs until the batter is smooth.
2. Place a large nonstick skillet over medium heat. Spray the skillet with cooking spray and add a heaping spoonful of the pancake mixture. Add batter to make 2 or 3 more pancakes (however many your pan will fit comfortably), then cook until the undersides are golden brown, 1 to 2 minutes. Gently flip (these are delicate!) with a spatula and cook for about 1 minute on the second side. Serve immediately or transfer to a platter and cover loosely with aluminum foil to keep warm. Repeat with the remaining batter, adding more cooking spray to the skillet as needed before each batch. Serve warm, with maple syrup, sliced bananas, sliced strawberries, coconut flakes, and/or peanut butter, if you'd like.

~~ *variations* ~~

PROTEIN BOOST
Whisk 2 teaspoons protein powder and 2 tablespoons smooth peanut butter into the batter.

HONEY ALMOND
Whisk 1 tablespoon almond flour into the batter. Serve with honey.

CHOCOLATE
Stir ¼ cup chocolate chips into the batter.

CINNAMON
Whisk ¼ teaspoon ground cinnamon into the batter.

No-Banana-Left-Behind Bread

BEST FOR when your roommate threatens to toss your brown bananas.

MAKES ONE 9 BY 5-INCH LOAF
ACTIVE TIME: 15 minutes
TOTAL TIME: 1 hour 15 minutes
LEVEL: Easy

Be the friend who knows what to do when someone (or yourself) lets their bananas turn black. Cooking this recipe from heart is beyond simple, so say hello to your new best banana friend.

½ cup vegetable oil, plus more for greasing

2 cups all-purpose flour

1 teaspoon baking powder

1 teaspoon baking soda

½ teaspoon kosher salt

2 large eggs

1 cup sugar

1 teaspoon ground cinnamon

1 teaspoon vanilla extract

4 very ripe bananas, mashed

1. Preheat the oven to 350ºF. Grease a 9 by 5-inch loaf pan with vegetable oil.

2. Combine the flour, baking powder, baking soda, and salt in a medium bowl. Whisk the eggs and sugar in a separate large bowl, then stir in the oil, cinnamon, vanilla, and banana. Stir in the flour mixture, one-third at a time, until just combined (some lumps are okay).

3. Pour the batter into the prepared pan. Bake until the crust is firm and dark golden brown, about 1 hour, or until an instant-read thermometer inserted into the center of the bread registers between 190º and 210ºF. Let cool for 15 minutes, then turn out onto a wire rack or plate and let cool completely.

#SPOONTIP If you're into nuts or grew up eating nutty 'nana bread, stir in ½ cup of your favorite kind. Nostalgia, ya know?

Chocolate-Hazelnut Banana Rolls

BEST FOR when you're the parent of the group and want to make something sweet.

SERVES 2
ACTIVE TIME: 10 minutes
TOTAL TIME: 10 minutes
LEVEL: Easy

When your friends come over for a night in, surprise them with these nuggets of goodness (plus wine or whatever drink you're feeling) instead of a bowl of candy or popcorn.

Vegetable oil, for frying

4 egg roll wrappers

1 egg, beaten

½ cup chocolate-hazelnut spread, such as Nutella

2 bananas, sliced

Confectioners' sugar, for dusting

Vanilla ice cream, for serving

1. Heat 1 inch of vegetable oil in a medium skillet over medium-high heat.

2. Lay an egg roll wrapper on your work surface and brush the edges with the beaten egg. Spread 2 tablespoons of the chocolate hazelnut spread in the middle of the wrapper, then add some banana slices (about 9 per roll) on top. Fold one side of the wrapper over the bananas and tuck in the top and bottom like a burrito (the beaten egg will help it stick together). Repeat with the remaining wrappers and filling.

3. When the oil is sizzling hot (an instant-read thermometer should register 350°F), fry the rolls until golden brown, turning them frequently, about 3 minutes. Transfer to a paper towel-lined plate, then dust with confectioners' sugar and serve with ice cream.

#SPOON TIP Cover egg roll wrappers with a damp dish towel or paper towel so they don't dry out while you're preparing.

MAKE-AHEAD MEALS THAT'LL UPGRADE YOUR LIFE

We believe that knowing how to meal prep like a champ should be listed on your résumé as a superpower. Even if planning ahead isn't your jam, we're gonna make this as painless as possible. Get the recipes that'll last in your pantry or the freezer from us, and we'll let you geek out on all the container options at the store. Welcome to the new world of preparedness.

Portable Veggie Egg Muffins

MAKES 12 MUFFINS
ACTIVE TIME: 10 minutes
TOTAL TIME: 35 minutes
LEVEL: Easy

Trying to make eggs before you run out the door for the day can be stressful—unless you embrace the muffin pan your mom passed down to you and use it to bake your eggs ahead of time.

Nonstick cooking spray

12 large eggs

Kosher salt and freshly ground black pepper

1 cup shredded Cheddar cheese

1 large tomato, chopped

½ small onion, chopped

Large handful of baby spinach, chopped

1. Preheat the oven to 350°F. Spray a 12-cup muffin tin with cooking spray.

2. Beat the eggs in a large bowl and season with salt and pepper. Add the Cheddar, tomato, onion, and spinach and stir to combine.

3. Pour the egg mixture into the muffin cups and bake until the muffins puff and are cooked through, about 25 minutes.

4. Let your egg muffins cool, then freeze them in a zip-top bag for up to 1 month. Microwave them for 1 to 2 minutes for a quick, handheld breakfast.

Goodbye, Hanger Trail Mix

MAKES 4¼ CUPS
ACTIVE TIME: 5 minutes
TOTAL TIME: 5 minutes
LEVEL: Easy

This is an easy trail mix that's great to have on hand during busy times of the year (deadlines, exams, snacking in general). Extra points if you make little baggies for your friends who are still students.

1 cup sweetened coconut chips, toasted

1 cup dried cranberries

¾ cup dried apricots, thinly sliced

½ cup roasted almonds

½ cup chocolate-covered raisins

½ cup salted roasted peanuts

Mix the coconut, cranberries, apricots, almonds, raisins, and peanuts together in an airtight container and store at room temperature for up to 1 month.

Go-To Turkey Chili

SERVES 4
ACTIVE TIME: 20 minutes
TOTAL TIME: 30 minutes
LEVEL: Easy

Chili is one of those dishes that's perfect to make a ton of: we never tire of eating it, even after day three when we move the rest of it to the freezer. Not only does this recipe use one of our favorite proteins, but you'll be done making it in half an hour. Huzzah.

2 tablespoons vegetable oil

1 green bell pepper, coarsely chopped

1 small onion, coarsely chopped

1 pound ground turkey

Kosher salt

1 tablespoon tomato paste

2 tablespoons chili powder

1 teaspoon ground cumin

1 (28-ounce) can diced fire-roasted tomatoes

3 cups low-sodium chicken broth

1 (15-ounce) can kidney beans, drained and rinsed

1 cup crushed tortilla chips, plus more for topping

Sour cream, shredded Cheddar cheese, pickled jalapeño, diced avocado, and/or finely chopped onion, for serving (optional)

1. Heat the vegetable oil in a large pot over medium-high heat. Add the bell pepper and onion and cook, stirring, until crisp-tender, about 4 minutes. Add the turkey and 1½ teaspoons of salt. Cook, breaking up the meat with a wooden spoon as it cooks, until cooked through, about 5 minutes. Add the tomato paste, chili powder, and cumin and cook, stirring, until the mixture darkens, about 1 minute.

2. Stir in the diced tomatoes, beans, broth, and crushed tortilla chips; bring to a simmer. Partially cover and cook, stirring occasionally, until thickened, 10 to 12 minutes. Season with salt. Ladle into bowls and top with more crushed tortilla chips, sour cream, Cheddar cheese, pickled jalapeño, avocado, and more onion, if you'd like.

#SPOON TIP This recipe can easily be doubled for a crowd. Just make sure to cook the vegetables and turkey a little longer.

#SPOONTIP The more you chop dates, the stickier they get, which makes these balls hold together better.

Balls of Energy

MAKES ABOUT 24 BALLS
ACTIVE TIME: 10 minutes
TOTAL TIME: 10 minutes
LEVEL: Easy

You could buy some sort of protein-granola product, or you could roll your own heavenly protein balls. Store them in an airtight container in the fridge for breakfast or pack them up to bring with you for a midday snack. Either way, you'll save some cash money and know exactly what you're eating. Win-win.

CHOCOLATE-MINT ENERGY BALLS

1 cup old-fashioned rolled oats

1 cup packed, finely chopped pitted dates

1 cup chopped chocolate

1/4 cup coconut oil

1/4 cup ground flaxseeds

16 crushed peppermint candies

Combine the oats, dates, chocolate, coconut oil, flaxseeds, and candies in a large bowl and mix well. Using damp hands, roll the mixture into 1½-tablespoon balls and set them on a plate. Refrigerate until firm.

CRANBERRY-COCONUT ENERGY BALLS

1 cup old-fashioned rolled oats

3/4 cup almond butter

1 cup dried coconut flakes

1/2 cup ground flaxseeds

1/4 cup dried cranberries

1/4 cup honey

Combine the oats, almond butter, coconut, flaxseeds, cranberries, and honey in a large bowl and mix well. Using damp hands, roll the mixture into 1½-tablespoon balls and set them on a plate. Refrigerate until firm.

PEANUT BUTTER-CHOCOLATE CHIP ENERGY BALLS

1⅓ cups old-fashioned rolled oats

3/4 cup creamy peanut butter

2/3 cup chocolate chips

1/2 cup ground flaxseeds

1/3 cup slivered almonds, chopped

3 tablespoons honey

Combine the oats, peanut butter, chocolate, flaxseeds, almonds, and honey in a large bowl and mix well. Using damp hands, roll the mixture into 1½-tablespoon balls and set them on a plate. Refrigerate until firm.

Minestrone Soup for Days

SERVES 6 TO 8
ACTIVE TIME: 35 minutes
TOTAL TIME: 45 minutes
LEVEL: Medium

This hearty soup is filled with all the good-for-you veg and filling pasta you could wish for. Make a large batch and store extras in the freezer for those lazy nights when you need comfort in a bowl.

2 slices bacon (2 ounces), chopped

¼ cup olive oil

5 garlic cloves, thinly sliced

3 medium carrots, coarsely chopped

2 celery stalks with leaves, coarsely chopped

1 medium onion, coarsely chopped

1 small head cauliflower (about 1½ pounds), broken into small bite-size florets

1 (28-ounce) can whole peeled tomatoes, drained and coarsely chopped

8 cups low-sodium chicken broth

⅓ cup ditalini, orzo, or other small pasta

1 (15-ounce) can kidney beans (or swap for any canned bean), drained and rinsed

1 (10-ounce) bag of frozen peas or cut green beans

½ cup grated Parmesan cheese, plus more for serving

Kosher salt and freshly ground black pepper

1. In a large pot, cook the bacon over medium heat until slightly crisp and the fat has rendered, about 4 minutes. Add the olive oil, garlic, carrots, celery, and onion. Cover and cook, stirring occasionally, until the vegetables soften, about 12 minutes.

2. Add the cauliflower, cover, and cook, stirring occasionally, for about 3 minutes more. Stir in the tomatoes and broth and bring to a boil. Stir in the pasta; reduce the heat to maintain a simmer and cook until the pasta is tender, about 12 minutes.

3. Add the kidney beans and frozen peas to the soup and cook, stirring, until heated through, about 3 minutes. Remove the soup from the heat and stir in the cheese. Season with salt and pepper.

Serve immediately, passing more cheese at the table. The soup will keep in the fridge for 3 days and in the freezer for 3 months.

#SpoonTip

MEAT-FREE: If you want to make this soup vegetarian, use vegetable broth and leave out the bacon.

FREEZING 101: Rule #1: Avoid putting hot things in the freezer, because it can cause other food to thaw and refreeze. Let it cool to room temperature first. **Rule #2:** Portion your food into useful servings before freezing. If you freeze it in a big block, you'll have to thaw the whole damn thing.

Green Enchiladas and Chill

SERVES 6 TO 8
ACTIVE TIME: 20 minutes
TOTAL TIME: 50 minutes
LEVEL: Easy

Coming home and not doing anything except switching into comfy pants and pushing some numbers on the microwave is usually our ideal night. This corn tortilla and green salsa enchilada is here to get you to that dream. You're welcome.

1 (15-ounce) can refried beans

16 ounces (4 cups) shredded Monterey Jack cheese

2¼ cups shredded rotisserie chicken (from about a ½ chicken; bones and skin discarded)

Kosher salt and freshly ground black pepper

1 (16-ounce) jar mild or medium green salsa

12 corn tortillas

Fresh cilantro leaves, chopped scallions, and sliced jalapeños, for serving (optional)

1. Preheat the oven to 375°F.
2. In a medium bowl, stir together the beans and 2 cups of the cheese. Fold the chicken into the bean mixture and season with salt and pepper.
3. Combine the salsa and 1 cup of water in a bowl, then pour 1 cup of the mixture into a 9 by 13-inch baking dish and spread it to cover the bottom.
4. Stack the tortillas and wrap them in damp paper towels; microwave until warm and pliable, about 15 seconds.
5. Arrange the tortillas on a work surface, then divide the chicken filling among them (use about ¼ cup of the filling per tortilla). Roll the tortillas up like cigars, then transfer them to the baking dish, seam-side down, positioning them so they fit snugly in the dish.
6. Pour the remaining salsa mixture over the rolled tortillas, then sprinkle with the remaining 2 cups cheese. Bake the enchiladas until the cheese melts and the enchiladas are hot in the center, about 30 minutes. Serve with cilantro, scallion, and jalapeños, if you'd like. Freeze individual portions in airtight containers and reheat them in the microwave when you're ready to eat.

THE GROUP DINNER CONUNDRUM

Potlucks are no longer synonymous with Midwestern mothers and congealed casseroles. Potlucks, or "group dinners," as we like to call them, are the end to your woes when it comes to eating with more than five people without spending all your cash. There's a way to divide and conquer the menu so everyone gets enough food and no one gets pegged with making every last ounce of it. Here's the formula for the food, but don't forget to BYOB, or see our Big-Batch Drinks starting on page 200.

Bacon-Wrapped Dates

MAKES 24 DATES
ACTIVE TIME: 10 minutes
TOTAL TIME: 30 minutes
LEVEL: Easy

Impress your crew by bringing over savory-sweet bacon-wrapped dates. Consider prepping them at home and bringing the pan to the party to cook them on the spot.

24 large pitted dates, preferably Medjool

12 slices bacon, halved crosswise

¼ cup maple syrup

Special equipment: 24 toothpicks

Preheat the oven to 425°F. Wrap each date with a piece of bacon and secure the bacon to the date with a toothpick. Space the dates evenly on a rimmed baking sheet and bake, turning the dates halfway through, until the bacon is golden and crisp, 18 to 22 minutes. Brush the dates with the maple syrup and bake until sticky, about 2 minutes more. (Use a paper towel if you don't have a basting brush.) Serve warm or at room temperature.

Disappearing Spinach-Artichoke Dip

MAKES 4 CUPS
ACTIVE TIME: 10 minutes
TOTAL TIME: 10 minutes
LEVEL: Easy

Make this creamy artichoke dip with frozen veggies and serve it straight out of the microwave. Use store-bought pita chips for the perfect group dinner dish that says "I tried but not that hard."

1 (10-ounce) package chopped frozen spinach, thawed

1 (10-ounce) package frozen artichoke hearts, thawed and chopped into pea-size pieces

1 (8-ounce) package cream cheese

¾ cup grated Parmesan cheese

¼ cup sour cream

½ teaspoon sriracha, or a few dashes of your favorite hot sauce

Pinch of garlic powder

Kosher salt

Pita chips, for serving

1. Microwave the spinach and artichokes in a microwave-safe bowl until hot, about 4 minutes. Let sit until cool enough to handle. Squeeze out the liquid with your hands.

2. In another large microwave-safe bowl, microwave the cream cheese until hot and soft, about 1 minute. Stir in the Parmesan, sour cream, sriracha, garlic powder, the spinach and artichokes, and ¾ teaspoon salt; serve hot with the pita chips.

#SPOON TIP Chill the finished dip and bring it to the party. When you get there, just reheat it in the microwave for 3 to 5 minutes, stirring a few times, until hot.

Spicy Parmesan Twists

MAKES 22 TO 24 STRAWS
ACTIVE TIME: 20 minutes
TOTAL TIME: 30 minutes
LEVEL: Medium

Turn two sheets of frozen puff pastry into the best bready appetizer you could ever want. Witchcraft? Nah, just cheese.

2 sheets frozen puff pastry (one 17.3-ounce box), thawed according to the package directions

All-purpose flour, for dusting

1 large egg

2 cups grated Parmesan cheese or shredded Cheddar cheese

1 teaspoon kosher salt

½ teaspoon red pepper flakes

1. Preheat the oven to 375°F. Line a baking sheet with parchment paper.
2. Roll out each sheet of puff pastry on a lightly floured work surface until it's 10 by 12 inches. Beat the egg with 1 tablespoon of water in a small bowl. Brush the entire surface of the pastry with the egg wash. Sprinkle each sheet evenly with 1 cup of the Parmesan, ½ teaspoon of the salt, and ¼ teaspoon of the red pepper flakes. With the rolling pin, lightly press the flavorings into the pastry. Cut each sheet crosswise with a floured knife or pizza wheel into 11 or 12 strips. Twist each strip a few times and lay it out on the prepared baking sheet.
3. Bake until lightly browned and puffed, 10 to 15 minutes. Turn each straw and bake for 2 minutes more. Don't overbake them, or the cheese will burn. Cool and serve at room temperature.

#SPOON TIP These are fragile, so take care not to crush them in transport. Wrap them in parchment paper or put them in large zip-top bags, then transfer them to an empty cereal box to protect them.

My Big Fat Greek Salad

SERVES 4
ACTIVE TIME: 15 minutes
TOTAL TIME: 15 minutes
LEVEL: Easy

The hardest part about eating salad is figuring out a mixture of healthy stuff that tastes like you're getting a full meal. When you can't think of your own combo and need to please a crowd, remember this recipe list for a Greek salad and you'll be set. Not feeling the olives? Skip 'em. The rules are yours to make.

GREEK SALAD DRESSING:

1 cup olive oil

6 tablespoons freshly squeezed lemon juice (from about 3 lemons)

1½ teaspoons dried oregano

2 garlic cloves, minced

Kosher salt and freshly ground black pepper

GREEK SALAD:

1 small red onion, cut into ½-inch wedges

1 head romaine lettuce (about 1 pound), trimmed of tough stems and torn into bite-sized pieces

8 ounces crumbled feta cheese

1 cup pitted kalamata olives

1 cup cherry tomatoes, quartered

1 English (seedless) cucumber, cut into 1-inch chunks

1 small green bell pepper, seeded and diced

1. For the Greek salad dressing: Put the olive oil, lemon juice, oregano, garlic, salt, and black pepper in a glass jar or plastic container with a tight-fitting lid. Shake until combined. (Makes 1½ cups; refrigerate for up to 1 week.)

2. For the Greek salad: Soak the onion in cold water for 5 minutes; drain. Toss the lettuce with ½ cup of the Greek salad dressing in a bowl. Divide the lettuce among 4 plates. Scatter the cheese, olives, tomatoes, cucumber, bell pepper, and drained onion over the lettuce.

#SPOON TIP Serve with warmed pita triangles or chips for your guests to use as a vehicle for the veg. Also, when you dress a salad, you want the lettuce to be shiny but still crisp. Add a little at a time. You can always add more but you can't undo.

Honey-Sriracha Brussels Sprouts

SERVES 8 TO 10
ACTIVE TIME: 10 minutes
TOTAL TIME: 40 minutes
LEVEL: Easy

This sweet-and-spicy take on Brussels sprouts is a rite of passage that puts your childhood ignorance of this glorious veggie behind you.

3 pounds Brussels sprouts, trimmed and halved lengthwise

¼ cup olive oil

Kosher salt

½ cup honey

1 tablespoon sriracha

1. Preheat the oven to 450°F.
2. Toss the Brussels sprouts with the oil in a large bowl. Season with salt.
3. Divide the Brussels sprouts between two rimmed baking sheets and spread in an even layer. Roast, rotating the baking sheets and tossing the Brussels sprouts halfway through, until crisp-tender and golden, 25 to 30 minutes.
4. Stir together the honey and sriracha in a small bowl. Remove the baking sheets from the oven and immediately drizzle each with half the honey mixture; toss to coat. Serve warm.

#SPOONTIP If Brussels sprouts aren't your thing, make this side dish with broccoli or cauliflower florets.

Party Kebabs

SERVES 8
ACTIVE TIME: 1 hour
TOTAL TIME: 1 hour 50 minutes
(includes marinating time)
LEVEL: Easy

Chop up some chicken, sausage, and veg, and you're halfway to the perfect party food. These epic kebabs will make sure everyone gets all the things, and they are super easy to stick in the oven to feed a big crowd.

1 medium red bell pepper, cut into 24 (1-inch) pieces

1 medium orange bell pepper, cut into 24 (1-inch) pieces

1 red onion, cut into 48 (1-inch) pieces

½ pineapple, cut into 24 (1-inch) chunks

1 pound chicken tenders, cut into 24 (1-inch) pieces

1 (14-ounce) package kielbasa, cut into 24 (½-inch-thick) rounds

½ cup teriyaki sauce

1 tablespoon honey

Kosher salt and freshly ground black pepper

Juice of ½ lime

Toasted shredded coconut and chopped fresh cilantro, for serving

Special equipment: 8 wooden skewers

1. Soak 8 wooden skewers in water for 30 minutes, then drain.
2. Make a kebab: Thread 1 red pepper piece, 1 orange pepper piece, 1 pineapple chunk, 2 onion pieces, 1 chicken piece, and 1 kielbasa piece (through the middle of the round) onto a skewer. Push the ingredients down to the end of the skewer. Repeat, in the same order, two more times, but thread the last piece of kielbasa through the edge of the round so that the kielbasa covers the pointed tip of the skewer. Repeat with the remaining ingredients to make 8 skewers total.
3. Whisk together the teriyaki sauce and honey in a baking dish. Add the kebabs and gently roll each skewer around to coat. Cover and refrigerate for 30 minutes.
4. Meanwhile, preheat the oven to 400°F. Line a rimmed baking sheet with aluminum foil.
5. Arrange the kebabs on the prepared baking sheet and drizzle the sauce from the baking dish over them. Sprinkle each side of the kebabs with salt and pepper. Bake until the chicken is cooked through and the peppers are soft, 20 to 25 minutes.
6. Drizzle the kebabs with the lime juice. Use your fingers to crush up the coconut into smaller pieces and sprinkle it over the kebabs. Sprinkle with cilantro.

Laid-Back Neapolitan Ice Cream Pie

SERVES 8
ACTIVE TIME: 15 minutes
TOTAL TIME: 2 hours 35 minutes
(includes freezing time)
LEVEL: Easy

If someone assigned you to be in charge of dessert, say no to just picking up a package of cookies. You don't even have to turn on the stove to make this pie, so you have no excuse for not pulling this one off.

2 cups Neapolitan ice cream

¾ cup smooth peanut butter

2½ cups crispy rice cereal

6 strawberries, halved, quartered, or sliced

1. Let the ice cream sit out at room temperature to soften, about 20 minutes.

2. In a large microwave-safe bowl, microwave ½ cup of the peanut butter in 30-second intervals, stirring after each, until warm and very loose, about 2 minutes. Add the cereal and toss until combined. Press the mixture into the bottom and up the sides of a 9-inch pie plate or foil pan.

3. Scoop the ice cream into the peanut butter crust and smooth it out into an even layer.

4. Microwave the remaining ¼ cup peanut butter in a small microwave-safe bowl until warm and loose, about 1 minute. Use a fork to drizzle the peanut butter over the pie.

5. Loosely cover with plastic wrap and freeze until set, at least 2 hours or up to overnight. Decorate with strawberries before serving.

#SPOON Tip If you're bringing this pie to a friend's, keep it in the freezer until right before leaving for the party and use a cooler or soft insulated bag to transport.

DATE NiGHT FOR THE HOPELESS ROMANTiC

Dating is weird. No matter where you live or how old you are, if you're trying this thing called companionship in the age of dating apps, we so understand the struggle. BUT if it hasn't happened to you yet, one day you'll meet a human you want to do more with than sit next to in a bar. Cooking with your significant other can actually be super fun and not painfully cheesy. Read on for the beginner's guide to having an epic time in the kitchen with your person.

Roll Your Own Sushi

SERVES 2
ACTIVE TIME: 40 minutes
TOTAL TIME: 1 hour
LEVEL: Boss

No need to spend all your money on soosh, or even buy one of those fancy kits. Learn how to make three types of sushi with your bare hands using simple ingredients in your kitchen like canned tuna, peanuts, and sriracha. Don't worry, we've included a raw fish hand roll for those die-hards out there.

SUSHI RICE:

1 cup sushi rice, rinsed

Kosher salt

1 tablespoon unseasoned rice wine vinegar

1 teaspoon sugar

SPICY TUNA ROLLS:

1 (5-ounce) can tuna (preferably oil-packed), drained

2 tablespoons mayonnaise

2 teaspoons sriracha

¼ teaspoon toasted sesame oil

2 sheets nori, toasted

½ ripe avocado, pitted, peeled, and thinly sliced

¼ small English cucumber, cut into long, thin matchsticks

Toasted sesame seeds or furikake seasoning (optional)

SWEET POTATO ROLLS:

1 small sweet potato, peeled and sliced lengthwise into 8 wedges

1 tablespoon honey

1 tablespoon low-sodium soy sauce

¼ small English cucumber, cut into long, thin matchsticks

¼ cup honey-roasted peanuts, lightly crushed

1 scallion, chopped

2 sheets nori, toasted

HAND ROLLS:

½ cup chopped sushi-grade salmon or tuna (3 ounces)

1 scallion, chopped

½ teaspoon vegetable oil

½ teaspoon toasted sesame oil

½ teaspoon sesame seeds, toasted

1 sheet nori, toasted and halved crosswise

½ ripe avocado, thinly sliced

Soy sauce, preferably low-sodium, for serving

Wasabi and pickled ginger, for serving (optional)

#SPOONTIP To make nigiri, form 2 tablespoons of sushi rice into a mound in your wet hand. Place it on a work surface and top with a thin slice of fish.

RECIPE CONTINUES

1. **MAKE THE RICE FIRST:**
Combine the sushi rice, 1¼ cups of water, and ½ teaspoon salt in a small pot. Bring to a boil, reduce the heat to maintain a simmer, cover, and cook for 15 minutes. Remove the pot from the heat and let stand, covered, for 15 minutes.

2. Combine the vinegar and sugar in a small microwave-safe bowl. Microwave until the sugar dissolves, about 30 seconds. Stir the vinegar mixture into the warm rice. Let cool, uncovered.

SPICY TUNA ROLLS

1. **MAKE THE SPICY TUNA ROLLS:**
Mix the canned tuna with the mayonnaise, sriracha, and sesame oil in a small bowl. Place both sheets of nori, shiny-side down, on a work surface. Using damp hands, spread ½ cup of the sushi rice in a horizontal strip in the center of each sheet, leaving a 1-inch border on the top and bottom and an ⅛-inch border on both sides. Divide the tuna mixture between the sheets and spread it in a strip evenly across the center of the rice on each nori. Divide the avocado and cucumber and place them horizontally next to the tuna. Sprinkle with sesame seeds, if you'd like.

2. Working with one sheet at a time, wet the top ¼ inch of the nori by dabbing a finger in a cup of cold water. Starting with the side closest to you, roll the bottom of the nori up over toward the top and continue to roll until you reach the end, pressing evenly to ensure the roll holds together. Lightly wet the outside of the seam to seal. Place the sushi roll seam-side down on a cutting board. Lightly wet a sharp knife and cut each roll crosswise into 8 pieces by first cutting it in half, then cutting each half in half, and finally cutting each piece in half again.

1. **MAKE THE SWEET POTATO ROLLS:**
Arrange the sweet potato wedges in a single layer on a microwave-safe plate and cover with a damp paper towel. Microwave until the wedges are tender, about 6 minutes. Remove the paper towel and let the wedges cool.

2. Meanwhile, combine the honey and soy sauce in a small microwave-safe bowl. Microwave until bubbling and thickened into a sauce, about 4 minutes. Let cool.

3. Place both sheets of nori, shiny-side down, on a work surface. Using damp hands, spread ½ cup of the sushi rice in the center of each sheet, leaving a 1-inch border on the top and bottom and an ⅛-inch border on both sides. Divide the sweet potato wedges, cucumber, peanuts, and scallion between the two sheets, placing them horizontally across the center of the rice. Drizzle the honey glaze over the toppings.

4. Working with one nori at a time, wet the top ¼ inch of the sheet by dabbing a finger in a cup of cold water. Starting with the side closest to you, roll the bottom of the nori up over toward the top and continue to roll until you reach the end, pressing evenly to ensure the roll holds together. Lightly wet the outside of the seam to seal. Place each sushi roll seam-side down on a cutting board and cut it into 8 pieces as you did with the tuna roll.

1. **MAKE THE THE HAND ROLLS:**
   Mix the chopped fish, scallions, vegetable oil, sesame oil, and sesame seeds in a small bowl. Place both half sheets of nori shiny-side down on a work surface. Using damp hands, spread a small pile (about 2 tablespoons) of rice horizontally on the left half of each nori strip, leaving a ½-inch border. Divide the chopped fish mixture and avocado between the two sheets, placing them on top of the rice. Starting from the bottom left corner, roll each nori sheet into a cone shape. Using your finger, gently wet the seam to seal.

2. Arrange all the rolls on a platter and serve with soy sauce, and pickled ginger and wasabi, if you'd like.

Make Baby Dumplings

MAKES 20 DUMPLINGS
ACTIVE TIME: 30 minutes
TOTAL TIME: 1 hour 30 minutes
(includes chilling time)
LEVEL: Medium

Dumplings are the perfect thing to make when you're craving some Chinese food but would rather stay indoors with your person. These dumplings call for shrimp, but if you're still not on the shrimp train, you can always fill them with any meat/veggie combo you're currently digging.

DUMPLINGS:

1 large egg white

¾ pound large shrimp, peeled and deveined, tails removed, and finely chopped

2 scallions, chopped

1 tablespoon cornstarch

1 teaspoon unseasoned rice wine vinegar

¾ teaspoon toasted sesame oil

½ teaspoon sugar

½ teaspoon Worcestershire sauce

Kosher salt and freshly ground black pepper

20 round dumpling wrappers, thawed if frozen

2 tablespoons canola oil

DIPPING SAUCE:

2 tablespoons soy sauce

2 tablespoons unseasoned rice wine vinegar

1 scallion, chopped

1. For the dumplings: Lightly beat the egg white in a large bowl. Add the shrimp, scallions, cornstarch, vinegar, sesame oil, sugar, Worcestershire, ¾ teaspoon salt, and a pinch of pepper. Stir well until the mixture starts to thicken, about 1 minute; cover and refrigerate until very cold, about 1 hour.

2. Set 1 dumpling wrapper on a clean surface (keep the rest covered with a damp paper towel so they don't dry out). Stir the shrimp mixture, then scoop 1 heaping teaspoonful onto the center of the wrapper. Dab a finger in a cup of cold water and moisten the edges of the wrapper. Fold in half and press the edges together to seal; transfer to a baking sheet. Cover with a damp paper towel while you form the remaining dumplings.

3. Heat 1 tablespoon of the canola oil in a large nonstick skillet or cast-iron skillet. Add half the dumplings in a single layer. Cook the dumplings, without turning, until browned on the bottom, about 3 minutes. Add 1 cup of water and bring to a boil. Reduce the heat to maintain a simmer, cover, and let the dumplings steam until fully cooked, about 5 minutes. Carefully transfer the dumplings to a serving plate and repeat with the remaining canola oil and dumplings.

4. For the dipping sauce: Combine the soy sauce, vinegar, and scallion in a small bowl. Serve with the dumplings.

#SPOON TIP The dumplings can be assembled and refrigerated the night before, too.

TURN PAGE FOR HOW-TO

how to make dumplings

Woo Them with Steak

SERVES 2
ACTIVE TIME: 15 minutes
TOTAL TIME: 50 minutes
LEVEL: Medium

Even if you eat this on $5 ceramic plates, that sprig of rosemary oozes class. No matter what type of potato or veggie you pair this with, making this date-night classic with your boo thang in your apartment always wins out over waiting at a white linen table.

1 (1-pound) boneless rib-eye steak, about 1 inch thick

Kosher salt and freshly ground black pepper

1 tablespoon olive oil

1 tablespoon unsalted butter

1 garlic clove

A few sprigs of fresh thyme or rosemary (optional)

Flaky sea salt, such as Maldon, for serving

1. Take the steak out of the fridge about 30 minutes before cooking it to bring it to room temperature so it cooks evenly.

2. Heat a large skillet over medium-high heat until very hot, about 2 minutes. (Cast iron is ideal because it retains heat and gives a great sear.) Pat the steak dry and generously season with kosher salt and pepper.

3. Heat the olive oil in the hot skillet, and when it just begins to smoke, add the steak. Reduce the heat slightly and cook the steak, untouched, until browned on the bottom, about 4 minutes. Flip the steak and cook for another 4 minutes or so for medium-rare (an instant-read thermometer inserted into the center of the steak from the side will register 125°F). During the last minute of cooking, add the butter, garlic, and fresh herbs to the skillet, tilt it toward you, and, using a spoon, ladle the melted butter over the top of the steak.

4. Transfer the steak to a cutting board and let it rest for 10 minutes so the juices distribute and don't run out of the steak when you slice it. Slice the steak across the grain, sprinkle with flaky salt, and serve.

#SPOON TIP Rib-eye is a nicely marbled cut, which means it stays juicy as the fat melts into the meat as it cooks. Other good options: NY strip or flat-iron steaks.

Chocolate Cake for Two

SERVES 2
ACTIVE TIME: 25 minutes
TOTAL TIME: 2 hours 25 minutes
(includes cooling time)
LEVEL: Medium

This cake recipe is the real MVP when it comes to date night, 'cause when you cut into it, it creates two perfect slices for you and your person. Dig into this velvety wedge, lovebirds.

CAKE:

Nonstick cooking spray

½ cup all-purpose flour

½ cup granulated sugar

¼ cup unsweetened cocoa powder

¼ teaspoon baking powder

¼ teaspoon baking soda

⅛ teaspoon kosher salt

⅓ cup buttermilk

⅓ cup hot water

1 large egg, at room temperature

½ teaspoon vanilla extract

FROSTING:

10 tablespoons (1¼ sticks) unsalted butter, at room temperature

6 tablespoons unsweetened cocoa powder

½ cup confectioners' sugar

Pinch of kosher salt

3 ounces semisweet chocolate, chopped and melted in the microwave

1. For the cake: Preheat the oven to 350°F. Line a 9-inch round cake pan with parchment and spray with cooking spray.

2. Whisk together the flour, granulated sugar, cocoa powder, baking powder, baking soda, and salt in a large bowl. Add the buttermilk, hot water, egg, and vanilla. Beat with a hand mixer on low speed or by hand until just combined. Increase the speed to medium and beat until smooth and well combined, stopping once to scrape down the bowl, about 2 minutes more.

3. Pour the batter into the prepared pan, and bake until the cake is just beginning to pull away from the sides and a toothpick comes out with a crumb or two attached, 15 to 20 minutes. Cool the cake in the pan on a rack for 20 minutes. Turn the cake out of the pan, remove the parchment, and let cool completely on a wire rack,

#SPOON TIP If you don't have a wire cooling rack, put the pan on chopsticks or move a stovetop grate to the counter. You can also use a toaster oven rack or the rack from your oven—just sit it up on a skillet so the air can circulate underneath.

about 1 hour. (The cake will look thin, but don't worry.)

4. For the frosting: In a large bowl using a hand mixer, beat the butter, cocoa powder, confectioners' sugar, and salt until light and fluffy. Scrape down the bowl, drizzle in the melted chocolate, and beat until combined.

5. To assemble: Quarter the cooled cake so you have 4 equal wedges. Frost the top of each wedge with about 2 tablespoons of the frosting (an offset spatula helps spread the frosting evenly, though a butter knife works, too). Stack the frosted wedges on top of one another on a serving plate, resulting in a four-layer piece of cake. Frost all three sides of the cake with the remaining frosting to completely cover. Let sit for 30 minutes. Slice it in half and serve.

FAKE IT TILL YOU MAKE iT

We're talking about adulting. The word *adulting* is accurate, yet moderately annoying—as is life, when you get a real job and have things to do. The plus side is that getting older means discovering new things and having the money to try them. So, if boxed booze, canned tuna, and cheese cubes are the only wine, seafood, and cheese options you can relate to, you're in the right place to expand your horizons and feel confident ordering at a restaurant. Plus, we've tossed in some legit recipes you'll need to impress your S.O. or your parents when they visit.

HOW TO BE A CONFIDENT HUMAN AT A NICE RESTAURANT

Eating at a restaurant (especially an expensive one) can feel like a less-than-chill experience. It's equivalent to trying to eat a full stack of ribs while holding your drink in your aunt's white living room that doesn't feel lived in. You don't want to mess up, but you also really want that meat. Here are some common scenarios and our advice on how to approach them.

YOUR WAITER POURS A SMALL AMOUNT OF WINE INTO YOUR GLASS AND STEPS BACK TO WATCH.

Don't freak out. Your server is asking you to try the wine to make sure it hasn't gone bad during fermentation, shipping, or storage—not to make sure it tastes good. If it tastes funky, you can politely send the wine back. It happens.

However, you should always take advantage of this somewhat awkward moment. Use this opportunity to actually enjoy and appreciate your wine! Swirl it, sniff it, and sip it just like you see in the movies. Maybe one day you'll start to notice the hints of lavender in your Pinot Grigio, or maybe it'll always just taste like wine. Which is still great.

YOU'RE WAY TOO STUFFED TO HAVE A FULL DESSERT, BUT YOU DON'T WANT THE MEAL TO END QUITE YET.

Many dessert menus also have a drinks section. Here you'll find sweet and strong liqueur options like grappa or other digestifs (which literally aid digestion). Friendly warning: Some of these can be quite strong, so drink your water, friends. If you're not a drinker, order a cup of coffee or tea to stick around and chat with your dinner friend.

YOU OR YOUR FRIEND HAVE A CUTE-ASS DOG AND YOU DON'T FEEL LIKE RUNNING HOME TO DROP IT OFF.

We like pets, you like pets, but maybe the person sitting at the table next to you just doesn't, or is allergic. If your dog isn't truly a service or therapy dog, it can prevent other dogs from doing their jobs if it makes a normal puppy mistake, like barking at strangers. If possible, have a date with your dog elsewhere or call ahead and see if they allow dogs outside.

YOU ORDERED A DRINK AT THE BAR, BUT NOW YOUR TABLE IS READY.

In most places, you can simply bring your drink with you. It's usually expected (and sometimes required) to close out your tab and tip for that drink at the bar to ensure that the bartender is receiving the tip. Even if you're also getting drinks at your table, you should still tip at the bar for that drink.

YOU HAVE A FOOD ALLERGY AND YOU FEEL AWKWARD ASKING FOR A SPECIAL REQUEST OR LETTING THEM KNOW ABOUT IT.

Don't be nervous to speak up for what's best for your body! If you truly have a food allergy, you don't want to mess around with that. Some staff might not be as used or equipped to make one-off changes, but more and more, restaurants are becoming more empathetic and accommodating to food allergies and all kinds of dietary restrictions.

YOU'RE STARING AT THE WINE MENU ON A DATE AND YOU'RE SUDDENLY FEELING NAUSEATED BECAUSE YOU HAVE NO IDEA WHAT TO CHOOSE.

Ask (*clap*) your (*clap*) waiter (*clap*). There's a time and place to be stressed, and the wine menu is not one of them. Your waiter or the restaurant's som-melier can point you in the right direction and give you a pairing that'll work with your entrée. Feel free to be specific about how much you want to spend on a bottle of wine. If you're afraid that "reasonably priced" or "on the low end" is too vague or lame, give the waiter a price range.

YOU ONLY ORDERED DRINKS, SO YOU'RE DEBATING A TIP.

Whether you're at an actual bar or you're sitting down and only got drinks—several people were involved in the service of those boozy, refreshing drinks, and they absolutely deserve a tip. Tip price can depend on where you are, but if you're standing at a casual bar, $1 a drink is a good place to start. However, if you're sitting at a table, we'd tip 20% out of courtesy to your server, especially if it's a full-service restaurant and you didn't order food.

YOU DIDN'T GET WHAT YOU ORDERED OR ARE OVERALL SUPER PEEVED BY YOUR EXPERIENCE.

Mistakes happen. A lot of people are involved in your order from the moment you sit down to the check, so whatever happened probably isn't one person's fault, and yelling at the server usually won't help the situation. Also, keep in mind where you're eating. If you're at a super-expensive restaurant, sure, the service should be nearly flawless, but if you're at a local pizza joint, being flexible and understanding is key.

THE SERVER-PATRON RELATIONSHIP YOU NEVER KNEW ABOUT: DOS AND DON'TS

We talked to some friends, siblings, and community members who have bussed and served at real restaurants to get their advice, and they all agreed that a simpatico relationship between the diner and server is a key part of having an enjoyable meal. Below are the 4 most important rules to consider that will not only make your dining experience better, but your server's as well.

1. **Eye contact and a smile go a long way.** No matter how hard it is for you to decide between the spaghetti and the rigatoni before the rest of the table finishes ordering, your server is likely more stressed than you are. Dealing with dozens of people from dozens of different backgrounds every night is nerve-racking and scary. Help your server feel more comfortable with your table by acknowledging their presence when they introduce themselves to the table. Look them in the eye and smile. Servers are humans! Nobody likes to be ignored.

2. **Kill them with kindness.** Again, if any part of your dining experience doesn't meet your standards, don't take it out on your server. The entire restaurant staff works together to provide you with an enjoyable dining experience, and mistakes can happen at any point between the time you enter the restaurant and when you pay your bill. Screaming at the restaurant staff might feel like justice is served, but it definitely doesn't make you any friends. Be polite when expressing your dissatisfaction and you might just win yourself a free drink or dessert on the house. Restaurant staff will be a lot more generous to diners who react positively to mistakes than those who don't. There's a strong "you-rub-my-back-and-I'll-rub-yours" mentality in restaurants.

3. **Servers love cash tips!** Paying the bill with a credit card is absolutely acceptable, but servers love when diners leave cash tips. That's money they can put in their pocket and take home right after their shift. If you have some cash in your pocket and you liked your service, leaving the tip in cash is a small extra gesture to say "thank you."

4. **Communication is key.** If you need a few extra minutes to make a menu decision, tell your server to come back; don't make them wait on you while you peruse all the items. They have things to do. Once you order, you can ask to keep a menu at your table if you think you might want to order more. However, be prepared that whatever you order in the middle of your meal might take longer than you expect. Additionally, don't forget to communicate with your waiter when you want your food to be served. Even though that salad is an entrée, clarify you want it to come out with the appetizers.

Carbonara That Brings the Heat

SERVES 4 TO 6
ACTIVE TIME: 15 minutes
TOTAL TIME: 30 minutes
LEVEL: Easy

Nothing says "I am an adult" like cooking with raw eggs. Get ready to learn how to make this classic dish with a much-appreciated spicy twist.

Kosher salt and freshly ground black pepper

8 ounces cubed pancetta

2 tablespoons olive oil

2 red or green jalapeños, halved, seeded, and thinly sliced

3 garlic cloves, thinly sliced

1 pound spaghetti

4 large eggs

1 cup grated Parmesan cheese, plus more for serving

1. Bring a large pot of salted water to a boil.
2. Cook the pancetta, olive oil, and jalapeños in a large skillet over medium heat, stirring occasionally, until the pancetta is crisp, about 10 minutes. Add the garlic and cook, stirring, until the garlic just turns golden, about 2 minutes. Remove from the heat and set aside.
3. Add the spaghetti to the boiling water and cook according to the package directions.
4. Whisk the eggs with the cheese and ½ teaspoon pepper in a large bowl. Drain the pasta, reserving ½ cup of the cooking water.
5. Return the skillet with the pancetta to medium-high heat. Add the pasta to the skillet and toss until heated through, 1 to 2 minutes. Remove from the heat. Whisk the reserved pasta water into the egg mixture.
6. Quickly scrape the warm pasta and pancetta mixture into the egg mixture, and toss to gently cook the eggs and make a creamy sauce. Serve immediately, with more Parmesan cheese.

#SPOON TIP Pre-cubed pancetta (unsmoked Italian bacon) is sold in grocery stores in 4-ounce packages, so buy two packages for this recipe. If you can't find it, it's fine to use chopped bacon instead.

Roast Chicken Power Move

SERVES 4
ACTIVE TIME: 25 minutes
TOTAL TIME: 6 hours 15 minutes
(includes chilling time)
LEVEL: Medium

We do not recommend roasting an entire chicken every single week for meal prep. However, we do implore you to know *how* to roast a chicken. That way, when you welcome your parents into your apartment for the first time, instead of saying, "Here's my nonexistent living room," you can make a grand arm gesture and say, "Here's this gorgeous meal I've prepared for you."

1 (3- to 4-pound) chicken

Kosher salt and freshly ground black pepper

2 tablespoons unsalted butter, at room temperature

1 teaspoon chopped fresh thyme, plus 1 sprig

1 teaspoon chopped fresh rosemary, plus 1 sprig

1 lemon, halved

1 small onion, halved

3 garlic cloves, smashed

1. Pat the chicken dry and set it on a large plate. Generously season the skin and inside the cavity with salt and pepper. Refrigerate, uncovered, for at least 4 hours or up to overnight to dry out the skin (this will make it nice and crispy). Let stand at room temperature for 30 minutes before roasting.

2. Preheat the oven to 425°F. Combine the butter, chopped thyme, and chopped rosemary with your fingers or a fork in a small bowl. Gently slide your fingers under the chicken skin on the breasts and legs to loosen it. Scoop up some of the herbed butter with a spoon; slide the spoon under the skin and hold the skin in place while you remove the spoon, leaving the butter behind. Smooth the skin to distribute the butter. Repeat with the remaining butter.

3. Squeeze the lemon juice into the cavity, then stuff the lemon halves inside the cavity. Stuff the onion, garlic, rosemary sprig, and thyme sprig into the cavity as well. Set a rack in a large roasting pan; put the chicken on the rack and roast until the skin is golden brown and an instant-read thermometer inserted into the thigh registers 170°F, 1 hour to 1 hour 15 minutes. When you slice into the meat, the juices should run clear.

4. Transfer the chicken to a platter and let rest about 10 minutes before carving.

HOW NOT TO BE AFRAID OF SEAFOOD

Ah, the fancy seafood issue. We've broken down the five most common bougie seafoods and listed some even more confusing seafood words for you, too, so you can feel fearless the next time something fishy is staring back at you.

OYSTERS

Oysters can be super polarizing: you love them, hate them, or think they taste like nothing. Personally, we think they're epic: they're served on a half-shell that they make themselves, on a bed of ice with seaweed. What could be bad about that?

To eat them the right way, all you gotta do is gently release the oyster from its shell with the small fork provided. They'll probably be served with lemon, cocktail sauce, and a thin, vinegary sauce called mignonette. Don't go too crazy on your garnish or you'll overwhelm the taste of the oyster (unless you're a beginner and you need all the garnishing help you can get). Pick up the shell and gently tilt the oyster into your mouth, juices and all. You can swallow it whole or chew it; both are perfectly normal.

LOBSTER

At fancier restaurants, lobster will come split lengthwise down the middle. Start with the big tail pieces, which can be eaten with a knife and fork and dipped into the melted butter (which the menu will probably call "drawn" butter). The claws and knuckles will typically already be cracked. If not, use the cracker that comes with your lobster and pull out the larger pieces with your fork.

At more casual places, the lobster will come whole. Tie on a plastic bib, roll up your sleeves, and get ready for some action. First start by grabbing the body in one hand and the tail in the other and twist to separate them. Squeeze the tail lengthwise together and then apart until it snaps. If that's not working, cut the underside of the shell with scissors. Continue by twisting off the claws where the knuckles attach to the bodies. Crack the claws just below the pincher. Try to apply pressure just to the shell, not the meat. You may need to crack it in several places to extract the meat in one piece. Pull the pincher backward until it cracks, then wiggle back and forth until it releases. The small sliver of meat should appear as you pull back the shell, but you may need to extract it with the lobster pick. For the knuckles, crack them in several places and then gently pull the meat out with your fingers or the lobster pick. These are delicious tender nuggets and are definitely worth the work. For the legs, you can break them off and suck out the meat, or skip it. Just don't forget to dip each morsel in the melted butter.

#SPOON TIP For the advanced lobster eater, pop off the top shell of the body and extract the greenish nugget called the tomalley. Although the FDA recommends not eating it because it can contain harmful toxins, connoisseurs believe it is the tastiest part.

SUSHI

ICYMI, sushi is meant to be eaten in one bite and has three traditional accompaniments: soy sauce, wasabi, and pickled ginger. Wasabi is quite hot and spicy, so a little goes along way. The pickled ginger is a palate cleanser and can be eaten at any time, just don't eat it with the sushi. Soy sauce is very salty, which you probably know, and should be used sparingly so it doesn't overpower the flavor of the fish. Pour the soy sauce into the tiny white bowl, dab in your preferred amount of wasabi, and stir. This is your dipping sauce for the rolls.

Maki are the rolls that are mostly associated with the word "sushi." These consist of dried seaweed and rice rolled around a filling and are usually cut into 6 or 8 pieces. The "inside-out" rolls with rice on the outside are called uramaki. Then you have nigiri and sashimi. Nigiri is a small mound of rice topped with raw fish, and sashimi is straight-up raw fish with no rice or seaweed. Best way to remember it: "S" as in solo.

MUSSELS

Try using an empty shell or a small seafood fork to delicately pluck a mussel from its shell. It's best to discard the shells into a separate bowl (usually the bowl that was used as a lid for the mussels) as you go. The broth at the bottom is good for dipping bread in or, better yet, French fries. The bottom of the broth can sometimes contain shell, sand, or grit, so as tempting as it is, don't drink the last few spoonfuls.

SHRIMP

When you order shrimp at a restaurant, it usually comes with most of the shell removed but the tail still on. This makes for a natural handle (thanks, shrimp!), but it's more than that: the tail also contains additional meat, so be sure to suck out the meat or twist off the tail to get the whole thing. For casual dining or appetizers such as shrimp cocktails, using your hands is perfectly acceptable. Shrimp dishes bathed in rich sauces require a fork and knife to remove the tails. Just push the tails to one side of your plate with your fork as you eat your shrimp.

OTHER FISH STUFF

Ordering a whole fish is a thing at nice restaurants, and they taste really damn good. If you're still easing into eating a fully scaled fish, you can ask your server to debone it, but there's a reason it's cooked with the bones in it. The flavor is epic, the skin is crispy, and the bones aren't too hard to pull out.

The last fishy thing we'll discuss for a hot second is raw fish. You ideally want fish to be frozen before you eat it raw, because that kills the bacteria. Still, eat at your own risk, because you can't always guarantee perfect prep.

Raw fish can come in plenty of shapes and sizes, but most typically you might see crudo or carpaccio. This means that whichever type of fish or seafood you're ordering will be served raw in very thin slices. Additionally, tartare is a super-popular menu item that refers to chopped-up raw meat with seasonings or a light sauce. Once you've tried raw fish, tuna tatare, take it up a notch and try steak tartare.

A Really Legit Shrimp Boil

SERVES 6
ACTIVE TIME: 30 minutes
TOTAL TIME: 30 minutes
LEVEL: Easy

Don't freak out: you *can* make this badass boil. Embrace this spicy one-pot recipe of potatoes, corn, and shrimp and make it a new tradition in your friend group every time it gets warm out.

2 lemons, halved, plus wedges for serving

½ cup seafood seasoning, such as Old Bay

6 garlic cloves

1 large red onion, quartered

½ teaspoon red pepper flakes

1 pound baby red potatoes

3 ears corn, husked and snapped in half

1 pound smoked sausage, such as andouille or kielbasa, cut into ½-inch slices

1 pound medium shrimp, peeled and deveined

4 tablespoons (½ stick) unsalted butter, melted

Hot sauce, for serving (optional)

1. Fill a large pot with 4 quarts of water. Add the lemon halves, seafood seasoning, garlic, onion, and red pepper flakes. Bring to a boil, then reduce the heat to medium to maintain a simmer and cook for about 5 minutes.

2. Add the potatoes to the pot and cook until just tender, about 10 minutes. Add the corn and sausage and cook for 5 minutes more. Add the shrimp, then cover and cook until the backs of the shrimp curl and the flesh turns opaque, 2 to 3 minutes.

3. Transfer the shrimp and vegetables to a large bowl with a slotted spoon or 2 spoons so the liquid stays in the pot. Drizzle with the butter and 1 cup of the broth. Serve with the remaining broth, lemon wedges, and hot sauce, if you'd like.

#SPOON TIP Make sure you have crusty bread to soak up this ridiculously good broth.

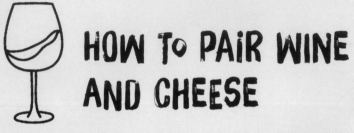

HOW TO PAIR WINE AND CHEESE

We realize that you're probably going to drink wine with other foods, too. However, pairing wine and cheese is actually super simple and a fun thing to get better at with practice. It feels fancy at first, then you'll get used to it and realize it's an epic alternative to going out for drinks and snacks.

START WITH THE WINE

When taking the next step from boxed grocery store wine (although, there are some amazing boxed wines out there), the best place to start is at a local wine shop. Wine geeks are usually super excited to educate people about wine, so tell them what you're looking for (even if that's "a bottle to take to a picnic") or that you're in need of a suggestion (like "to chase the Sunday scaries"). Don't be afraid to tell them you know nothing. Every wino has gotta start somewhere.

KNOWING WHAT TYPE OF CHEESE TO PAIR WITH THE WINE

When tasting wine, one of the first things to think about is body, which is a sensual term for the impact you get from the flavor of the wine. You'll know right away. When you taste the wine, does it hit you with a pow of flavor that lingers in your mouth, or is it subtle, light, and quick to disappear?

If it's the former (full bodied), you want to make sure you pair it with a cheese that also packs a punch. If it's the latter (lighter), make sure the cheese is also subtle. It's not that either are lacking flavor, it's that one is delicate and may call for a little extra concentration.

STILL CONFUSED?

Buy cheeses you like, and serve a crisp dry white wine and a light red wine (like Pinot Noir), because they tend to work with a lot of options. If serving a blue cheese, add a drizzle of honey over the top of the cheese to make it more approachable. And when in doubt, cheese and wines from similar regions taste better together. Try Rioja with Manchego, Comté cheese with an Alsatian white, or a light Tuscan red with pecorino.

IMPRESS YOUR CREW

When building a cheese board, think about flavor, texture, and color. Go with at least three to five different cheeses. Nuts, fruits, jams, and honeys also add elements of crunch, sweetness, and palate cleansing. Plus, they look good in photos. Finally, up your game by copying the French and serve cheese as dessert.

#SPOON TIP If your best friends from school are visiting, swap one of your nights on the town for a wine and cheese night. When you only have a handful of hours with your favorite people, actually being able to have a convo (and as much wine as you want) is key.

GENERAL RULES
FOR DAIRY + VINO
SUCCESS

1. Experiment: If you don't have any known faves, start with a variety of cheeses to discover new flavors and preferences: soft, hard, creamy, nutty, pungent, and tart. Some will be fresh cheeses and some will be aged—both are totally cool.

2. Order Matters: If you're tasting multiple cheeses and wines, start with the lightest first and work toward the more robust flavors. This will ensure that the light ones aren't overwhelmed by the strong ones.

3. Balance Is Key: When pairing, the goal is to complement, i.e., not to cover up the flavors of either the wine or the cheese. This can be done with similar flavors working together in unison or contrasting flavors to help to balance out the other. Think creamy Havarti paired with buttery Chardonnay for like flavors, or a strong blue evened out by a sweet port.

CHEESE PAIRINGS FOR
QUICK REFERENCE

WINE		CHEESE PAIRING
Bubbly	⟶	Parmigiano-Reggiano
Riesling	⟶	Blue Cheese
Dry Rosé	⟶	Chèvre
Chardonnay	⟶	Brie
White Bordeaux	⟶	Gouda
Pinot Noir	⟶	Gruyère
Cabernet Sauvignon	⟶	Aged Cheddar

Unpretentious Ratatouille

SERVES 6 TO 8
ACTIVE TIME: 1 hour 45 minutes
TOTAL TIME: 2 hours 15 minutes
(includes eggplant draining time)
LEVEL: Medium

The key to being the very best host is making something everyone wants to eat. We're here to tell you that the people want roasty, golden veggies. They just might not know it yet. If you're cooking for a guest with a bigger appetite, you can serve it with chicken or another protein on the side.

1 large eggplant, cut into 1-inch pieces

Kosher salt and freshly ground black pepper

8 tablespoons olive oil

4 red onions, cut into 1-inch pieces

4 garlic cloves, finely chopped

3 medium zucchini, cut into 1-inch pieces

1 red bell pepper, cut into 1-inch pieces

8 vine-ripened tomatoes, peeled, seeded, and cut into 1-inch pieces

4 sprigs rosemary

4 sprigs thyme

10 fresh basil leaves

1. Toss the eggplant with 1 tablespoon salt until well coated in a colander over a bowl. Cover the eggplant with a plate and weight it down with a plastic zip-top bag filled with water. After 30 minutes, remove the weight and plate and squeeze any remaining water from the eggplant by pressing it down against the colander with your hands.

2. Heat 2 tablespoon of the olive oil in a large skillet over medium heat. Add the onions and cook, stirring occasionally, until soft and golden, 10 to 12 minutes. Add the garlic and cook, stirring occasionally, for 5 minutes more. Transfer the mixture to a large bowl.

3. Heat 2 more tablespoons of the oil in the skillet and add the eggplant. Cook, stirring frequently, until golden and beginning to brown, 15 to 20 minutes. Transfer the eggplant to the bowl with the onions.

4. Heat 2 more tablespoons of the oil in the skillet and add the zucchini. Cook, stirring frequently, until golden, about 15 minutes. Transfer to the bowl with the other vegetables.

5. Heat the remaining 2 tablespoons oil in the skillet and add the bell pepper. Cook, stirring frequently, until soft, about 10 minutes.

6. Return all the vegetables to the skillet and add the tomatoes, rosemary, and thyme. Simmer for about 30 minutes. Remove the herb sprigs. Tear the basil leaves and stir them into the vegetables. Season with salt and black pepper. Serve warm or at room temperature.

#SPOON TIP Ratatouille tastes even better the next day—or the day after that. Keep it in an airtight container in the fridge for up to 1 week.

BIG-BATCH DRINKS FOR ALL YOUR PEOPLE

Even if you don't live somewhere with all four seasons, the passing of time gives everyone the feels. We're always looking forward to the next season, like snuggly nights by the fire or beachin' it with friends, and pairing a drink with your mood feels really damn good. We've mixed up something over the top for summer, cozy for winter, and everything in between. Make enough for your friends and celebrate the season or the reason. Cheers.

Suns Out, Margs Out

SERVES 8
ACTIVE TIME: 5 minutes
TOTAL TIME: 5 minutes
LEVEL: Easy

Here's how you can hack a classic margarita recipe for that first warm day in the year when you're really feeling those chill, sunshiny vibes.

2 cups tequila

½ cup frozen limeade concentrate

½ cup orange liqueur, such as Cointreau

2 limes, 1 halved and sliced and 1 cut into wedges

Ice

2 cups seltzer

Mix the tequila, frozen limeade, and orange liqueur in a large pitcher. Add the lime slices and stir to combine. Divide the mixture among 8 rocks glasses filled with ice. Add ¼ cup of the seltzer to each. Stir gently to combine. Garnish each glass with a lime wedge.

#SPOON Tip Up your game by rubbing the rims of your glasses with a lime wedge and dipping each in a plate of salt mixed with chile powder.

Summer Beer

SERVES 8 TO 10
ACTIVE TIME: 5 minutes
TOTAL TIME: 5 minutes
LEVEL: Easy

Send a friend out into the heat for beer, vodka, pink lemonade, and ice. Now follow these majestic instructions for the best adult beverage to kick off summer.

One 6-pack light summer beer (such as Corona)

1 (12-ounce) can frozen pink lemonade concentrate

12 ounces vodka

12 cups ice

Lemon slices, for serving

Mix the beer, lemonade concentrate, and vodka in a large pitcher. Stir to combine. Serve over ice with lemon slices.

#SPOON TIP Turn this into a boozy slushie by buzzing all the ingredients, including the ice, in a blender (you may have to do this in batches). For extra points, serve with umbrellas.

Fireball Sangria

SERVES 8 TO 10
ACTIVE TIME: 10 minutes
TOTAL TIME: 2 hours 10 minutes
(includes chilling time)
LEVEL: Easy

Use your go-to cinnamon whiskey to make this fall-forward sangria. This mixture is ideal for tailgates, autumn birthdays, and various other sweater-weather occasions.

1 (750-ml) bottle red wine, such as Cabernet Sauvignon

6 ounces cinnamon whiskey, such as Fireball

3 apples, quartered and sliced

3 oranges, halved and sliced

½ cup cranberries

1 (750-ml) bottle sparkling cider, chilled

Ice (optional)

Mix the red wine, whiskey, apples, oranges, and cranberries in a large pitcher. Stir to combine. Refrigerate for 2 hours. Add the sparkling cider; stir to combine. Serve in glasses with a bit of fruit in each. Add ice, if desired.

#SPOON TIP If you can't find Fireball, just use regular bourbon and add some cinnamon sticks to the mix.

Peppermint Schnapps Hot Cocoa

SERVES 16 TO 18
ACTIVE TIME: 15 minutes
TOTAL TIME: 2 hours 5 minutes
LEVEL: Easy

Don't let the winter blues get you down. This spiked cocoa made in the slow cooker will warm you up and keep your spirits high. Even when you're wearing an ugly sweater that hasn't been washed in three years.

3 cups confectioners' sugar, sifted

2 cups unsweetened cocoa powder

12 cups whole milk

2 teaspoons vanilla extract (optional)

1 teaspoon kosher salt

8 ounces dark chocolate, finely chopped

1 cup peppermint schnapps, plus more for serving

24 peppermint candies, crushed (about 1 cup)

3 cups mini marshmallows, for serving

1. Whisk the sugar and cocoa powder in a 6-quart slow cooker. Turn the cooker to High and slowly whisk in the milk. Add the vanilla (if using) and salt. Cover and cook for 1½ hours.

2. Whisk the chocolate into the milk mixture in the cooker, a little bit at a time, until it all melts. Replace the lid and cook on High until thickened, 30 minutes more.

3. Turn the cooker to Warm and stir in the schnapps. Ladle into mugs and serve with small bowls of the peppermint candies, mini marshmallows, and a small pitcher of schnapps alongside.

#SPOON TIP Serve with candy cane stirrers for extra holiday vibes.

OVER THE TOP, AND WE'RE INTO IT

Playing with your food is an art, and it can also get absolutely ridiculous.
Food porn cynics, we feel your pain. Bacon-wrapped everything is
unrealistic, and no one will ever really make that edible piñata mermaid
unicorn rainbow glitter cake-croissant galaxy coffee drink hybrid. But
like . . . they're also really freaking cool. Whether you actually eat these
or not, here's how you can make the next food sensation *and* make your
friends go "well that's a little ridiculous." Get at us.

Epic PB&J Chocolate Cup

SERVES 10 TO 12
ACTIVE TIME: 30 minutes
TOTAL TIME: 50 minutes (includes freezing time)
LEVEL: Medium

Follow your childhood heart song and whip up this giant PB&J chocolate cup for literally any celebration, whether your BFF got a new job or your roommate finally cleaned the apartment.

Nonstick cooking spray

2 (11.5-ounce) bags milk chocolate chips

1½ cups smooth peanut butter

¾ cup confectioners' sugar

½ cup finely crushed saltine crackers (about 10)

3 tablespoons unsalted butter, at room temperature

Kosher salt

1 cup grape jelly

10 to 12 mini chocolate-coated peanut butter cups, such as Reese's

Special equipment: 9-inch tart pan with removable bottom

1. Spray the tart pan with cooking spray. Melt the chocolate in a large heatproof bowl set over—not in—a pot of simmering water, making sure the bottom of the bowl does not touch the water.

2. Pour half the melted chocolate into the prepared pan. Freeze until the chocolate is set and hardened, about 10 minutes. Keep the remaining chocolate warm in the bowl over the pot on low heat until ready to use.

3. Meanwhile, combine the peanut butter, confectioners' sugar, saltines, butter, and a pinch of salt in a large bowl and blend with a hand mixer on medium speed until well combined (or stir really well with a mixing spoon). Spread the peanut butter mixture over the chocolate in the pan with an offset spatula or butter knife, leaving a ½-inch border around the edge. Spread the jelly on top of the peanut butter mixture with the offset spatula.

4. Pour over the remaining melted chocolate, spreading it over the top so it drips into the open border and no filling is visible. Freeze until set, about 15 minutes.

5. Reserve 1 tablespoon of the remaining ½ cup peanut butter in a small microwave-safe bowl. Drizzle over the peanut butter cup. Transfer the remaining peanut butter to a small zip-top bag. Snip ¼ inch off one corner and pipe 10 to 12 small dots of peanut butter around the edge of the peanut butter cup. Press a mini peanut butter cup on top of each dot. Serve at room temperature.

Party in Your Mouth Pineapple Bowls

SERVES 4 TO 6
ACTIVE TIME: 1 hour
TOTAL TIME: 1 hour
LEVEL: Medium

Out-of-this world presentation paired with chicken that tastes like your favorite takeout = true love. But first, let's talk about the mad props you'll get for carving out that amazing pineapple bowl.

1 small pineapple

6 tablespoons canola oil

1½ cups long-grain rice

Kosher salt and freshly ground black pepper

3 tablespoons soy sauce

1 tablespoon distilled white vinegar

2 tablespoons cornstarch

1 pound boneless, skinless chicken breasts, cut into 1-inch pieces

1 medium onion, chopped

½ red bell pepper, cut into ½-inch-wide strips

2 cups broccoli florets

2 garlic cloves, chopped

1 tablespoon chopped or grated fresh ginger

2 teaspoons sesame oil

2 teaspoons sesame seeds, for garnish

1. Halve the pineapple lengthwise, then scoop out the inner flesh, leaving a ½-inch border. Cut out and discard the core of the pineapple. Chop the flesh into ½-inch pieces; set aside 1½ cups. Reserve the remaining flesh for another use. Trim off a small piece of the skin on the bottom of each half so the bowls sit flat.

2. Heat 2 tablespoons of the canola oil in a medium pot. Add the rice, stir, and cook until toasted, about 2 minutes. Add 3 cups of water and 2 teaspoons of salt and bring to a boil. Stir and reduce the heat to maintain a simmer. Cover and cook for 12 minutes. Remove from the heat and let stand, covered, for 5 minutes. Fluff with a fork and keep warm until ready to serve.

3. Combine the soy sauce, vinegar, and 3 tablespoons of water in a small bowl. In another small bowl, stir together 2 tablespoons of water and the cornstarch until all the lumps have dissolved. Set aside.

4. Heat 2 tablespoons of the canola oil in a large skillet over high heat. Season the chicken with salt and black pepper. When the oil starts to shimmer, add the chicken to the pan; cook until the chicken is browned on all sides, about 4 minutes. Transfer the chicken to a plate.

5. Add the remaining 2 tablespoons canola oil; when the oil starts to shimmer, add the onion and bell pepper and cook, stirring, until the vegetables soften, about 4 minutes. Add the broccoli and cook until crisp-tender, about 4 minutes. Add the garlic and ginger and cook, stirring, until fragrant, about 1 minute. Add the chopped pineapple and the soy sauce mixture and bring to a boil. Add the cornstarch mixture, return to a boil, then reduce the heat to maintain a simmer; cook, stirring occasionally, until slightly thickened, about 5 minutes.

6. Return the chicken to the pan and stir until the chicken is coated. Add the sesame oil and remove from the heat. Serve in the pineapple bowls with the cooked rice and garnish with sesame seeds.

The Most Extra Donut Cake Ever

SERVES 6
ACTIVE TIME: 30 minutes
TOTAL TIME: 6 hours 30 minutes
(includes chilling time)
LEVEL: Boss

This confectionary creation doesn't involve baking at all. Round up some store-bought donuts and turn them into a coffee-chocolate masterpiece.

1 (3.9-ounce) package chocolate pudding mix (plus the ingredients called for on the package)

1½ cups heavy cream

½ cup sugar

1 tablespoon vanilla extract

18 assorted cake donuts

7 ounces brewed coffee, warm

2 tablespoons jarred chocolate sauce

¼ cup mini chocolate chips

1. Prepare the pudding according to the package directions.
2. Whip the heavy cream, sugar, and vanilla in a medium bowl with a hand mixer on medium speed until the cream holds stiff peaks, about 3 minutes.
3. Line a baking sheet with parchment paper. Slice the donuts in half horizontally so you have 36 round halves. Place 6 halves on the prepared baking sheet, cut-side up, so you have three rows of two donuts each. Drizzle 1 teaspoon of the coffee over each of the donuts. Spread ¼ cup of the pudding over the donuts, then ¼ cup of the whipped cream. Place 6 more donuts on top, cut-side down, and repeat the process four more times. Place the remaining 6 donut halves cut-side down on top. Spoon the remaining pudding into the center of each donut. Spoon the remaining whipped cream into the spaces between the donuts. Drizzle with the chocolate sauce and sprinkle with the chocolate chips.
4. Refrigerate for 6 hours or up to overnight before serving.

#SPOON TIP Use a serrated knife to easily slice the donuts without breaking them into pieces.

Smiley Fries for a Bad Day

SERVES 4
ACTIVE TIME: 35 minutes
TOTAL TIME: 35 minutes
LEVEL: Medium

This smiley fry recipe is one of our top performing videos of all time (with well over 100 million views), so we wanted to memorialize it in this cookbook and encourage you to try it yourself. Major nostalgia and DIY vibes coming up next.

2 medium russet potatoes, peeled and cut into 1-inch pieces

Kosher salt and freshly ground black pepper

¼ cup all-purpose flour, plus more for dusting

3 tablespoons bread crumbs

3 tablespoons cornstarch

1 large egg, lightly beaten

1 (48-ounce) bottle canola oil

Ketchup, for serving

1. Put the potatoes in a medium pot, cover with water by at least 1 inch, and season the water generously with salt. Bring to a boil, then reduce the heat to maintain a simmer. Cook until the potatoes are soft, about 15 minutes. Drain the potatoes and transfer to a large bowl. Add the flour, bread crumbs, cornstarch, and egg. Mash everything with a fork until the potato mixture forms a dough. Season with 2 teaspoons salt and 1½ teaspoons pepper.

2. Roll out the dough between two pieces of parchment paper to ¼ inch thick. Carefully peel off the top piece of parchment. Cut out 1½-inch circles, using the rim of a glass. Using the end of a drinking straw, cut out two small circles for the eyes and use a spoon to cut out a mouth.

3. Heat the canola oil in a large pot over medium-high heat until it measures 350ºF on a deep-fry thermometer. If you don't have one, test the oil by adding a pinch of the potato dough: if it starts to sizzle and brown, the oil is ready. Working in batches, transfer the smiley fries to the oil with a spatula and cook until golden brown and crispy, 2 to 4 minutes, flipping halfway through. Transfer to a paper towel–lined plate and sprinkle with salt. Repeat with the remaining smiley fries. Serve with ketchup.

No-Sharing-Required Mason Jar Banana Split

SERVES 1
ACTIVE TIME: 10 minutes
TOTAL TIME: 1 hour 10 minutes
(includes freezing time)
LEVEL: Easy

Here's a homemade, single-serve dessert that has some mad social media potential. Just pick your filter, cheeky caption, and post.

1 brownie

1 scoop vanilla ice cream

1 banana, sliced into ¼-inch rounds

1 scoop chocolate ice cream

1 scoop strawberry ice cream

2 tablespoons chocolate sauce

Whipped cream, for serving

1 maraschino cherry

Rainbow sprinkles, for serving

Special equipment: 1 wide-mouth mason jar, 2-inch ice cream scoop

1. Freeze the mason jar until very cold, about 1 hour. Cut half the brownie into six ½-inch cubes. Place the vanilla ice cream in the bottom of the mason jar. Top with 3 pieces of brownie and a few slices of banana. Top with the chocolate ice cream, 3 more pieces of brownie, and more banana slices. Top with the strawberry ice cream. Drizzle with the chocolate sauce and top with the remaining banana slices.

2. Cut the remaining half brownie into a triangle and stick it on top of the strawberry ice cream. Top with whipped cream, the cherry, and some sprinkles.

Tater Tot Waffle Grilled Cheese

* MIC DROP *

SERVES 1 OR 2
ACTIVE TIME: 15 minutes
TOTAL TIME: 15 minutes
LEVEL: Easy

Did you really think we'd get through this whole book without incorporating Tater Tots? We wouldn't do that to you. Enjoy these cheesy tots in a brand-new form.

1 (32-ounce) bag frozen Tater Tots

4 slices Cheddar cheese

4 slices cooked bacon

2 tablespoons pickled jalapeño slices (optional)

Special equipment: waffle iron

Preheat the waffle iron. Completely cover the bottom plate of the waffle iron with a snug, even layer of Tater Tots, 30 to 32 total. Close the lid and cook until golden brown and crispy, about 10 minutes. Transfer the waffled tots to a plate and repeat to make a second one. Leaving the second waffle in the waffle iron, layer on the cheese, bacon, and jalapeño (if using). Place the first waffle on top, close the lid, and cook until the cheese has melted, 2 to 3 minutes.

ACKNOWLEDGMENTS

Written by Rachel Williamson
Photography by Andrew Purcell
Mackenzie Barth
Monica Pierini
Stephanie Hanes
Cameron Curtis
Jill Novatt

Heather Ramsdell
Lygeia Grace
Dana Bowen
Vince Camillo
Mary Beth Bray
Chanel Betuk
Jenny Bierman

Leah Brickley
Angela Carlos
Liza Cohen
Ginevra Iverson
Laura Rege
Liza Zeneski

Spoon University is a digital food media brand and community that helps you build your confidence in becoming a real adult. Below is a list of amazing current and graduated students who contributed their recipes to our cookbook. We couldn't have done this without you all—we love you more than we love toast:

ASHLEIGH DE SIMONE	Curry Chicken Salad
MAX FAUCHER	Toasted Ramen Avocado Slaw
RAYNA MOHRMANN	Empty Peanut Butter Jar Noodles
MARIS ROSENFELD	Scrappy Cream Cheese Pasta
PHOEBE MELNICK	Penne alla Leftover Vodka
KATHERINE RICHTER	Loaded Shrimp Nachos
SARAH SILBIGER	BBQ Chicken Sweet Potato Meets Avocado Whip
SABRINA MARQUES	Badass Brown Butter Gnocchi
ALVIN ZHOU	Mediterranean Toast
MIKAYLA BAIOCCHI	Desperate Times Pizza Toast
ALEX FRANK	No-Bread Sweet Potato Toast
BECKY BLAIR	BEC Oatmeal
NICK SCHMIDT	Straight-Up Banana Ice Cream
ZOE ZAISS	2-Ingredient Flourless Pancakes
HELENA LIN	Chocolate-Hazelnut Banana Rolls
CAITLYN HETER	Portable Veggie Egg Muffins
JAMIE COHEN AND ALEXIS CLIFFORD	Balls of Energy
SHALYANE PULIA	Party in Your Mouth Pineapple Bowls
ARDEN SARNER	Tater Tot Waffle Grilled Cheese, Smiley Fries for a Bad Day
ELENA BESSER	For all of the recipe ideas everywhere

One million kudos go out to the Spoon University HQ team for their support; to our families and friends; to Vikki Neil and Kathleen Finch; to Caroline O'Toole for her creative eye; and to our larger Food Network, Scripps, and Discovery family; and to our community for years of curiosity, inspiration, and taking risks.

INDEX

Copyright © 2018 by Spoon Media Inc., a subsidiary of Discovery, Inc.

All rights reserved.
Published in the United States by Harmony Books, an imprint of the Crown
Publishing Group, a division of Penguin Random House LLC, New York.
crownpublishing.com

Harmony Books is a registered trademark, and the Circle colophon is a trademark
of Penguin Random House LLC.

Library of Congress Cataloging-in-Publication Data
Title: How to feed yourself : 100 cheap, easy, fast, and good recipes for cooking
when you don't know what you're doing.
Description: First edition. | New York : Spoon University / Harmony Books, 2018.
| Includes index.
Identifiers: LCCN 2018015472 (print) | LCCN 2018019115 (ebook) | ISBN
9780525573746 (ebook) | ISBN 9780525573739 | ISBN 9780525573746
    (ebook)
        Subjects: LCSH: Quick and easy cooking. | LCGFT: Cookbooks.
        Classification: LCC TX833.5 (ebook) | LCC TX833.5 .C65263 2018
        (print) | DDC 641.5/12—dc23
        LC record available at https://lccn.loc.gov/2018015472

                ISBN 978-0-525-57373-9
                Ebook ISBN 978-0-525-57374-6

                Printed in China

                Book and cover design by SONIA PERSAD
                Cover and interior photography by ANDREW PURCELL

                10 9 8 7 6 5 4 3 2 1

                First Edition